OPPOSING
VIEWPOINTS®
SERIES

Chemicals

Other Books of Related Interest:

Opposing Viewpoints Series
Endangered Oceans

Energy Alternatives

The Environment

Natural Gas

Scientific Research

At Issue Series
Biological and Chemical Weapons

Genetically Modified Food

Animal Experimentation

Current Controversies Series
Gasoline

Pesticides

Pollution

"Congress shall make no law ... abridging the freedom of speech, or of the press."

First Amendment to the US Constitution

The basic foundation of our democracy is the First Amendment guarantee of freedom of expression. The Opposing Viewpoints series is dedicated to the concept of this basic freedom and the idea that it is more important to practice it than to enshrine it.

Chemicals

Margaret Haerens, Book Editor

GREENHAVEN PRESS
A part of Gale, Cengage Learning

GALE
CENGAGE Learning·

Farmington Hills, Mich • San Francisco • New York • Waterville, Maine
Meriden, Conn • Mason, Ohio • Chicago

GALE
CENGAGE Learning®

Patricia Coryell, *Vice President & Publisher, New Products & GVRL*
Douglas Dentino, *Manager, New Products*
Judy Galens, *Acquisitions Editor*

For more information, contact:
Greenhaven Press
27500 Drake Rd.
Farmington Hills, MI 48331-3535
Or you can visit our Internet site at gale.cengage.com

For product information and technology assistance, contact us at

Gale Customer Support, 1-800-877-4253
For permission to use material from this text or product, submit all requests online at www.cengage.com/permissions

Further permissions questions can be emailed to permissionrequest@cengage.com

Articles in Greenhaven Press anthologies are often edited for length to meet page requirements. In addition, original titles of these works are changed to clearly present the main thesis and to explicitly indicate the author's opinion. Every effort is made to ensure that Greenhaven Press accurately reflects the original intent of the authors. Every effort has been made to trace the owners of copyrighted material.

Cover Image copyright ©Jiri Vratislavsky/Shutterstock.com.

LIBRARY OF CONGRESS CATALOGING-IN-PUBLICATION DATA

Chemicals / Margaret Haerens, book editor.
    pages cm. -- -- (Opposing viewpoints)
    Includes bibliographical references and index.
    ISBN 978-0-7377-7248-7 (hardcover) -- ISBN 978-0-7377-7249-4 (pbk.)
    1. Pollution--Environmental aspects. 2. Hazardous substances. 3. Pollutants. I. Haerens, Margaret.
    TD176.7.C474 2015
    363.738'4--dc23
                                           2014029439

Contents

Chapter 3: How Are Chemicals Endangering the Water and Food Supply?

Chapter 4: How Should the Government Protect Americans from Toxic Chemicals?

Why Consider Opposing Viewpoints?

> *"The only way in which a human being can make some approach to knowing the whole of a subject is by hearing what can be said about it by persons of every variety of opinion and studying all modes in which it can be looked at by every character of mind. No wise man ever acquired his wisdom in any mode but this."*
>
> *John Stuart Mill*

In our media-intensive culture it is not difficult to find differing opinions. Thousands of newspapers and magazines and dozens of radio and television talk shows resound with differing points of view. The difficulty lies in deciding which opinion to agree with and which "experts" seem the most credible. The more inundated we become with differing opinions and claims, the more essential it is to hone critical reading and thinking skills to evaluate these ideas. Opposing Viewpoints books address this problem directly by presenting stimulating debates that can be used to enhance and teach these skills. The varied opinions contained in each book examine many different aspects of a single issue. While examining these conveniently edited opposing views, readers can develop critical thinking skills such as the ability to compare and contrast authors' credibility, facts, argumentation styles, use of persuasive techniques, and other stylistic tools. In short, the Opposing Viewpoints Series is an ideal way to attain the higher-level thinking and reading skills so essential in a culture of diverse and contradictory opinions.

In addition to providing a tool for critical thinking, Opposing Viewpoints books challenge readers to question their own strongly held opinions and assumptions. Most people form their opinions on the basis of upbringing, peer pressure, and personal, cultural, or professional bias. By reading carefully balanced opposing views, readers must directly confront new ideas as well as the opinions of those with whom they disagree. This is not to argue simplistically that everyone who reads opposing views will—or should—change his or her opinion. Instead, the series enhances readers' understanding of their own views by encouraging confrontation with opposing ideas. Careful examination of others' views can lead to the readers' understanding of the logical inconsistencies in their own opinions, perspective on why they hold an opinion, and the consideration of the possibility that their opinion requires further evaluation.

Evaluating Other Opinions

To ensure that this type of examination occurs, Opposing Viewpoints books present all types of opinions. Prominent spokespeople on different sides of each issue as well as well-known professionals from many disciplines challenge the reader. An additional goal of the series is to provide a forum for other, less known, or even unpopular viewpoints. The opinion of an ordinary person who has had to make the decision to cut off life support from a terminally ill relative, for example, may be just as valuable and provide just as much insight as a medical ethicist's professional opinion. The editors have two additional purposes in including these less known views. One, the editors encourage readers to respect others' opinions—even when not enhanced by professional credibility. It is only by reading or listening to and objectively evaluating others' ideas that one can determine whether they are worthy of consideration. Two, the inclusion of such viewpoints encourages the important critical thinking skill of objectively evaluating an author's credentials and bias. This evaluation will illuminate an author's reasons for taking a particular stance on an issue and will aid in readers' evaluation of the author's ideas.

It is our hope that these books will give readers a deeper understanding of the issues debated and an appreciation of the complexity of even seemingly simple issues when good and honest people disagree. This awareness is particularly important in a democratic society such as ours in which people enter into public debate to determine the common good. Those with whom one disagrees should not be regarded as enemies but rather as people whose views deserve careful examination and may shed light on one's own.

Thomas Jefferson once said that "difference of opinion leads to inquiry, and inquiry to truth." Jefferson, a broadly educated man, argued that "if a nation expects to be ignorant and free . . . it expects what never was and never will be." As individuals and as a nation, it is imperative that we consider the opinions of others and examine them with skill and discernment. The Opposing Viewpoints series is intended to help readers achieve this goal.

David L. Bender and Bruno Leone,
Founders

Introduction

> "If we ever had proof that our nation's pollution laws aren't working, it's reading the list of industrial chemicals in the bodies of babies who have not yet lived outside the womb."
>
> —Louise Slaughter,
> US representative from Kentucky

On the morning of January 9, 2014, approximately 7,500 gallons of MCHM, a mildly toxic chemical coating agent, spilled into the Elk River, about a mile upstream from a major water intake and treatment center that provides drinking water to the city of Charleston, West Virginia. Authorities were alerted to the problem when people in the area noticed the overwhelming smell of licorice, a defining characteristic of MCHM, also known by its name 4-methylcyclohexane methanol. Complaints about the smell began pouring into the West Virginia Department of Environmental Protection (DEP) from all over the city and surrounding areas near the river.

A search into the source of the leak was launched, and a few hours later DEP investigators traced the smell to a coal processing plant owned by a company called Freedom Industries that was located on the Elk River. MCHM, which is used to strip impurities from coal processing, was streaming through cracks in a concrete containment dike, leaching into the ground and spilling into the river. Although officials at Freedom Industries were aware of the problem, DEP investigators reported that efforts to stop the spill were clearly inadequate—in fact, almost nonexistent. Thousands of gallons of the chemical already had contaminated the land and water.

Freedom Industries not only failed to alert DEP of the spill, but it also did not notify West Virginia American Water, a private company responsible for providing municipal water for parts of nine counties in and around the city of Charleston. By that afternoon, DEP informed the water company that a toxic chemical spill had occurred upstream from its water intake and processing plant, which filters water for drinking and other purposes. Within a few hours, the water company's officials realized that the plant's filtration system would not be able to handle the amount of contaminants in the water.

By late afternoon, approximately three hundred thousand residents living in the Charleston area were advised not to use the tap water for drinking, bathing, or washing. That meant that nearly 16 percent of West Virginians would be without water until the problem was fixed. Health officials warned residents that exposure to MCHM could cause headaches, eye and skin irritation, diarrhea, nausea, and respiratory problems. State officials were disturbed to learn that there had been little testing on MCHM's long-term health effects or its environmental impact.

A state of emergency was called on January 9 by Governor Earl Ray Tomblin, who also activated the National Guard to help with disaster response. That same day, President Barack Obama declared the chemical spill to be a national emergency and directed the Federal Emergency Management Agency (FEMA) to provide logistical and financial assistance for the state's emergency response efforts. The coordinated response included the distribution of hundreds of thousands of gallons of potable water.

Despite the warning and the strong taste of licorice from the MCHM in the water, many residents were affected from ingesting the chemical. It was reported that more than one hundred people had to seek treatment for nausea and vomiting, with about a dozen hospitalized. Businesses and schools in the area were forced to close. By January 13, residents in some areas were allowed to use the water again after taking some precautions, such as flushing water from their pipes and hot water tanks.

In the aftermath of the chemical spill, a number of federal and state agencies launched investigations into the incident. The US attorney in the region announced his intention to investigate the circumstances surrounding the spill and the response by Freedom Industries for criminal violations. Both the US Chemical Safety Board and the Occupational Safety and Health Administration launched investigations. Many health officials urged in-depth research into the long-term effects of MCHM on humans and the environment.

On February 12, a field hearing was held by the US House Committee on Transportation and Infrastructure in Charleston, West Virginia. It was the first federal hearing on the Elk River chemical spill and one of the first opportunities to bring different agencies, experts, and policy makers together to review the incident and focus attention on constructive ways to prevent such disasters in the future.

The chairman of the committee, Representative Bill Shuster, underscored the need for the hearing and for a full understanding of what had occurred. "It is critically important for this committee to be here today, to hear from the folks who have been on the ground since the spill occurred, and to gain an understanding of what happened in this incident," he maintained in his opening statement at the hearing. "I can only imagine how it has been for the residents of this region over the past month. The uncertainty and unanswered questions must be overwhelming at times. As Americans we should all feel safe to drink the water that comes out of our faucets. We should be able to take a shower without worrying what's in the water. We should have confidence that our governmental leaders are doing everything in their power to ensure the safety of our water supply. That is why we are here today."

The authors of the viewpoints in *Opposing Viewpoints: Chemicals* consider the threat of chemical exposure to public safety in chapters titled "What Threats Do Chemicals Pose to the Environment and Public Health?," "What Can Lead to

Dangerous Levels of Toxic Chemical Exposure?," "How Are Chemicals Endangering the Water and Food Supply?," and "How Should the Government Protect Americans from Toxic Chemicals?" The information presented in this volume provides insight into the health risks posed by exposure to chemicals found in plastics, cosmetics, and other products common in everyday life; examines the controversies surrounding e-cigarettes, pesticides, hydraulic fracturing, and chemical dispersants used in oil spills; and considers the efforts to reform the existing federal regulatory framework to protect the American public from toxic chemical exposure.

OPPOSING
VIEWPOINTS®
SERIES

CHAPTER 1

What Threats Do Chemicals Pose to the Environment and Public Health?

Chapter Preface

The United States has an obesity problem. According to the Centers for Disease Control and Prevention (CDC), more than one-third of all American adults are obese. It is also a problem among American youth, with the CDC estimating that 17 percent of children and teens aged two to nineteen are obese. If the current trends continue, experts believe that obesity rates for adults could reach or exceed 44 percent in every US state by 2030. These high rates have led many public health officials to be concerned that the nation is in the throes of an obesity epidemic, which poses serious health risks and economic costs.

As obesity rates continue to rise, a number of researchers have devoted resources to finding the reason for the disturbing epidemic. In 2012 then secretary of health and human services Kathleen Sebelius listed a few of the causes in a speech at the Weight of the Nation conference. "When we talk about our country's obesity epidemic, we're talking about a relatively recent development," she said. "And several factors came together all at once to create the steep rise in obesity that our country has seen over the last three decades."

One factor of the obesity epidemic is the chemicals prevalent in everyday modern life. Numerous scientific studies have found that endocrine-disrupting chemicals, such as bisphenol A (BPA), phthalates, and certain pesticides, interfere with the hormonal mechanisms that regulate body weight. In infants, these chemicals can turn certain cells into fat cells, which stay with the individual for life.

Many researchers believe that chemicals are the only reason for the rise in obesity among infants under six months. A 2006 Harvard School of Public Health study found that the prevalence of obesity in this demographic had risen 73 percent since 1980.

"The evidence now emerging says that being overweight is not just the result of personal choices about what you eat, combined with inactivity," suggests Retha Newbold, an official with the National Institute of Environmental Health Sciences (NIEHS). "Exposure to environmental chemicals during development may be contributing to the obesity epidemic."

Obesity is just one of several problems attributed to chemical exposure. The following chapter examines the threats that chemical exposure poses to public health and the environment. Other viewpoints in the chapter discuss the pervasive nature of chemicals in everyday life, whether the rising concern over chemical exposure is justified or exaggerated, and how chemicals affect different socioeconomic communities.

> "The troubling rise of autism, obesity, attention deficit hyperactivity disorder, type 2 diabetes and prostate and breast cancers in recent years has spread concern in the scientific community about the potential effects of low-dose exposure to hazardous chemicals such as BPA, especially early in life."

There Are Too Many Unregulated Chemicals in Everyday Life

Melinda Burns

Melinda Burns is a journalist and former staff writer for the Pacific Standard. *In the following viewpoint, she favorably assesses Carl F. Cranor's book* Legally Poisoned: How the Law Puts Us at Risk from Toxicants, *which argues that outdated laws place Americans at risk from untested industrial chemicals. Burns finds that ineffective US laws allow dangerous toxic chemicals to be put on the market without testing for potential health risks, turning Americans into guinea pigs for unregulated chemicals. Experts believe that exposure to toxic chemicals causes several health problems, including autism, cancer, and type 2 diabetes. Burns agrees with the Cranor's thesis that better regulation is needed to identify dangerous toxic chemicals before they hit the market and pose a threat to public health.*

As you read, consider the following questions:

1. According to Burns, how many environmental chemicals has the Centers for Disease Control and Prevention measured in the bodies of Americans since 1999?

2. How many industrial chemicals does the author contend the US Environmental Protection Agency requires to be tested after they are offered for sale?

3. In what year did the European Union begin requiring thirty thousand existing and new chemicals to be tested for potential health and environmental hazards?

Let's say you want to live a healthy life. You eat organic food to avoid pesticides, and you buy free-range chicken to steer clear of antibiotics. You stay away from swordfish because of the mercury warnings. You move out of the smoggy downtown.

But hard as you try, you will not be safe, says Carl F. Cranor, author of an unnerving new book, *Legally Poisoned: How the Law Puts Us at Risk from Toxicants.* Since 1999, the Centers for Disease Control and Prevention [CDC] has measured 219 environmental chemicals in the bodies of Americans. Most of the population carries around measurable levels of lead from automobile exhaust, flame retardants from carpets and epoxy resins in water bottles, like those pictured on the cover of Cranor's book. Most Americans over 20 have been exposed to PCBs [polychlorinated biphenyl], dangerous coolants that were formerly used in electrical transformers.

No amount of "self-help" can save people from being chemically invaded, Cranor says. A lawyer and philosopher by training, he straddles science and law at the University of California, Riverside, studying the convoluted and contradictory patchwork of U.S. regulations on toxics and carcinogens.

"It is simply morally outrageous to treat citizens as experimental subjects by contaminating them with untested substances," Cranor writes. "This stands in stark contrast to the way people are treated under the ethical guidelines for medical experiments and the laws concerning pharmaceuticals and pesticides." In a recent interview, he said the U.S. needs to recognize "this deep inconsistency."

A Dangerous Gamble

Drugs and pesticides undergo rigorous laboratory experiments before they can be sold, but there's almost no public data showing whether 82,000 industrial chemicals registered for sale in the United States were tested for potential health risks before entering the market, Cranor says. Because the Toxic Substances Control Act of 1976 doesn't require such testing, it effectively turns Americans into "guinea pigs for reckless free enterprise," he says: "I think it's a disastrous piece of legislation."

Instead of requiring manufacturers to conduct and pay for pre-market testing, Cranor says, the law puts the burden on the U.S. Environmental Protection Agency [EPA] to police the industry after products are offered for sale, opening the gates for companies to bog down the system with court challenges.

A Broken System

To date, the EPA has required post-market testing for only 200 industrial chemicals. In 1998, the manufacturers of 2,800 chemicals of high production volume, defined as more than 1 million pounds a year, agreed voluntarily to test their products for potential risks to humans and the environment, but the program has fallen far behind schedule. In this sort of enforcement system, few chemicals ever get the "death penalty."

It was Congress, not the EPA, that banned PCBs. Today, studies of laboratory animals suggest that flame retardants known as polybrominated diphenyl ethers, or PBDEs, found in carpets and chair cushions, may cause damage to the liver, thyroid and nervous system, especially in children. Two types of these chemicals were phased out in 2004, and the EPA has announced a voluntary phaseout of another type by the end of 2013, but they have not been banned.

Earlier this year, citing an "uncertain business environment" stemming from a "fundamental lack of confidence in our nation's chemicals management system," the head of the American Chemistry Council told a congressional committee that the industry was in favor of modernizing the Toxic Substances Control Act. But the council's proposals do not include broad pre-market testing. "If we didn't believe our products were already safe for their intended uses, we wouldn't be making them," Cal Dooley, the council president, said.

Legally Poisoned is a frightening book. It reminds readers that lead poisons the nervous system and PCBs disrupt the reproductive system and that both have a long half-life, afflicting both humans and the environment decades after lead was banned from gasoline and PCB use was outlawed. The book cites a number of studies on laboratory animals that suggest a link between adult disease and early exposure to ubiquitous chemical substances, including perfluorinated compounds [PFCs] in Scotchgard and nonstick cookware, and bisphenol A, or BPA, a synthetic estrogen that hardens the plastic in water bottles, baby bottles and the liners of cans.

The Counter Argument

Taking the opposite tack, another new book, *Scared to Death: How Chemophobia Threatens Public Health*, seeks to debunk these studies and reassure the public. Published as a "position statement" by the American Council on Science and Health, an industry-friendly nonprofit group, it says the "regulation of

About DES

Diethylstilbestrol (DES) is a synthetic estrogen that was developed to supplement a woman's natural estrogen production. First prescribed by physicians in 1938 for women who experienced miscarriages or premature deliveries, DES was originally considered effective and safe for both the pregnant woman and the developing baby.

In the United States, an estimated 5–10 million persons were exposed to DES during 1938–1971, including women who were prescribed DES while pregnant and the female and male children born of these pregnancies. In 1971, the Food and Drug Administration (FDA) issued a drug bulletin advising physicians to stop prescribing DES to pregnant women because it was linked to a rare vaginal cancer in female offspring.

More than 30 years of research have confirmed that health risks are associated with DES exposure. However, not all exposed persons will experience . . . DES-related health problems.

"About DES,"
Centers for Disease Control and Prevention, 2014.

chemicals is better and more effective than it's ever been," and chemicals used in consumer products "have undergone enough testing so that there is a reasonable likelihood that they will cause no harm when used properly." The book calls BPA "relatively innocuous" and questions whether studies on laboratory animals can be used to draw conclusions about risks to humans.

"The only significant science-based question is whether a particular substance is harmful at the trace levels to which humans are exposed," says author Jon Entine, a journalist and visiting fellow at the American Enterprise Institute, a conservative think tank in Washington, D.C.

A Feasible Theory

Nonetheless, the troubling rise of autism, obesity, attention deficit hyperactivity disorder, type 2 diabetes and prostate and breast cancers in recent years has spread concern in the scientific community about the potential effects of low-dose exposure to hazardous chemicals such as BPA, especially early in life. The concept of the "developmental origins of disease," based on animal studies and human data, has gained broad acceptance, and it supplies the underpinnings for Cranor's arguments in *Legally Poisoned*—the idea that many illnesses may develop through a series of "hits" or exposures to hazardous chemicals, beginning in the womb. In this view, an exposure to toxics during a critical developmental window early in life might alter how a person's DNA functions, leading to cerebral palsy, leukemia, dementia, Parkinson's or other maladies later on.

Cranor believes a less risky world is within reach. As an example, he points to the European Union, which in 2007 began requiring 30,000 existing and all new chemicals to be tested for potential health and environmental hazards. European manufacturers and importers must submit technical data on their products showing that they can be used safely, or they will be restricted or banned. The operative slogan is, "No data, no market."

Major Legislative Efforts

In the U.S., two groundbreaking bills—the Safe Chemicals Act and Toxic Chemicals Safety Act—were introduced by Democrats in the House of Representatives last year. Both would have required pre-market testing; both died without a vote. In the vacuum, 18 states have taken matters into their own hands, passing 71 chemical safety laws during the past eight years.

Some of these laws have banned BPA from baby and toddler products and phased out PBDEs in the home. In a recent example of "retail regulation," Wal-Mart Stores Inc. earlier this year banned PBDEs in hundreds of consumer goods, including couches, cameras and child car seats.

Among state laws, California's Proposition 65, a voter-approved initiative, is the strongest: It lists nearly 900 toxic substances (though not BPA or PBDEs) and requires companies to warn the public if their products contain them. Many companies have opted to take toxics off the market instead.

The American Chemistry Council says state and local governments lack the scientific expertise and resources to make such regulatory decisions. "In practice," Dooley, the council president, told members of Congress, "multiple state and local laws regarding chemicals create confusion among manufacturers, retailers and consumers, hamper the development of new products, close off markets, and ultimately prevent business growth and new hiring, all without significantly improving public safety."

Cranor disagrees: "As a tactic, I think we ought to encourage going jurisdiction by jurisdiction to deal with these problems. It's a headache for industry."

Legally Poisoned gets bogged down in the details of chemicals and their health effects, but its regulatory message comes through loud and clear. During a long career, Cranor has been an adviser to the Congressional Office of Technology Assessment and California's Proposition 65, and he has served on committees of the National Academy of Sciences and the Institute of Medicine. Along the way, he's been pulled into personal injury cases as an expert witness.

The Impact of the DES Daughters

But tort law cannot prevent contamination; it can only compensate people after they get sick. In his book, Cranor reviews the cautionary tale of the "DES daughters," one of the most egregious regulatory failures of the last century. Beginning in the 1970s, thousands of women in the U.S. were diagnosed with rare vaginal cancers and other disorders decades after their mothers took diethylstilbestrol [DES], a synthetic estrogen that was mistakenly believed to prevent miscarriages. The DES scandal prompted a huge wave of lawsuits against the manufacturers of the drug.

"The history of toxic contamination should worry us," Cranor says. "We have a world that's filled with industrial chemicals. We should recognize the seriousness of the problem and not wait for a catastrophe."

> *"Learning how to handle life's risks is critical to human development, and it would be a problem if parents failed to teach children how to assess risks on their own."*

Americans Cannot Be Paralyzed by Fear When It Comes to Chemical Exposure

Julie Gunlock

Julie Gunlock is a journalist, a conservative political commentator, an author, and the director of the Independent Women's Forum Culture of Alarmism project. In the following viewpoint, she derides the "culture of alarmism" that has permeated American society today and has led to a state of hysteria over everything from toxic chemical exposure to food labeling. Gunlock blames activist organizations that stoke fear and anxiety in parents by exaggerating dangers from chemicals and foods to extend the reach of government regulation into people's daily lives. Consumers often pay for the changes caused by overregulation of business. She urges American parents to calm down and rely on common sense instead of overreacting to every childhood danger, arguing that it is essential that children learn to assess dangers for themselves and manage the everyday risk associated with modern life.

As you read, consider the following questions:

1. According to the author, what dangerous chemical is found in polyvinyl chloride?

2. According to the Centers for Disease Control and Prevention (CDC), how many children under the age of four died of suffocation in 2011?

3. How many children does the CDC report go to emergency rooms every year because they fall and hurt themselves?

A few years ago, I was watching the news and was shocked to learn that my garden hose was incredibly dangerous.

Say, what?

The newscaster anchoring the program that night seemed really upset about this story. He leaned forward in his seat, stuttered . . . and . . . wait . . . did I see him tear up? Did his voice just crack? Oh my gosh, he's going to cry!

This.is.a.serious.problem.

SOMETHING MUST BE DONE! NOW!

It's weird. I sometimes fall for it. I know I shouldn't but sometimes . . . only once in a while . . . I forget and fall into the alarmist trap. These news anchors seem so eager to protect me, so gallant, with such nice hair and skin. They look like they smell really good and take care of their teeth. They are genuinely concerned for my kids. I think they like me. I bet they'd want to hang out. . . .

The Insidious Hand of Big Government

And then I snap out of it and remember that this is all part of the plan to freak me out so that I will welcome, even demand, the guiding hand of government. The alarmists and their media pals know that as a mom, I'm vulnerable to this type of messaging. They hope for this type of reaction: outrage, horror and fear.

Yet the real facts behind the "killer garden hoses lurking in your backyard" are hardly scary. The news story centered on the fact that most garden hoses are made of polyvinyl chloride, better known as PVC. PVC has high levels of lead and other chemicals and, therefore, the claim was that since children and pets sometimes drink from garden hoses, they were getting big doses of toxins when taking the occasional sip.

But before you read anymore, just think about it: Do children and pets really drink a lot of water from garden hoses? Is the garden hose a main source of water for children and pets? Are they drinking gallons of water this way?

Sure, during summer months, kids consume some "garden hose water" as they play in the sprinkler or splash in the kiddie pool. They may take a gulp or two when mom's watering the garden. But in general, kids do not get the bulk of their water in any given day—much less during their lives—from the garden hose. After all, the alarmists also tell us that kids drink too much juice and soda, and we know that doesn't come out of a garden hose.

Avoiding the Hysteria

I was lucky that I had time to look into this story and question its merits. I was able to ignore the hysteria, and consider the facts. And those facts are reassuring. Most garden hoses are indeed made of made of polyvinyl chloride, which is toxic if consumed in large quantities. Yet, it is impossible—let me repeat that word, *impossible*—for a human to consume enough water to reach toxic levels of PVC exposure. Why is this impossible? Because the amount of chemical that leaches into the water is so miniscule that a person would have to consume massive amounts of garden hose water in order for it to be a problem. And if a person attempted to drink the amount of water required to reach PVC toxicity, they'd first die of dilutional hyponatremia—death by water overdose—before reaching that toxic level.

In other words, you simply cannot poison yourself with garden hose water. You cannot harm yourself by the occasional sip of garden hose water. Again, it's impossible.

Alarmists naturally ignored this common sense and called for regulations on the garden hose industry. One terrified mommy blogger wrote: "I can't tell, looking at a hose, whether or not it is safe. Only a large scale overhaul of the regulations that govern what chemicals get into our stuff, such as the Safe Chemicals Act, can begin to protect us." But so far manufacturers of garden hoses have been allowed to carry on with their businesses without having to jump through any new regulatory hoops.

But this doesn't mean there isn't a cost. Right now there are moms out there who are sitting on patios watching their toddlers run through the sprinkler or jump in the kiddie pool who are filled with fear of their garden hose. You can almost envision the scene: Instead of just enjoying the moment watching their kids play and laugh and work off some energy, these moms are periodically stopping to pester junior not to drink through the hose. The kids probably won't listen and will drink the water anyway, so then mom will become angry and begin yelling.

Ultimately, she'll be left feeling defeated, worried, and scared. The kids will also feel bad, not enjoying the play as much and may even feel vaguely worried that they've endangered themselves. That may not impact the national economy, but it is making the country a worse place to live.

Stoking Anxiety

But these activist organizations don't seem to care that the anxiety level in this country is already off the charts. These groups understand that nervous parents are powerful allies in the effort to have manufacturers add warning labels to nearly every product they produce.

Yet, parents should also understand these warning labels come at a high cost to their bottom line because when the government mandates that a manufacturer alter its packaging or manufacturing practices, the costs associated with the changes aren't simply absorbed by the company. Rather, the costs are passed to consumers, most of whom never asked for these changes in the first place.

We Need a Warning Label on Warning Labels

And while the alarmists like to say, unreservedly, that nearly everything sold in the grocery stores should come with a large warning label—on the front of the package—reasonable parents know these labels do next to nothing to protect children, especially as warning labels become so ubiquitous people inevitably tune them out.

Consider what is now being labeled a threat to our children. In 2010, the American Academy of Pediatrics (AAP) announced that "high-risk" foods like apples, chewing gum, chunks of peanut butter, hard candy, marshmallows, nuts, popcorn, raw carrots, sausages, seeds, grapes, and hot dogs should come with a warning label. The idea wasn't that there were nutritional problems with these items, but the AAP wanted parents warned that these foods posed a choking hazard to young children.

But is choking as big a problem as the AAP portrays it to be?

According to the Centers for Disease Control [and Prevention, CDC], 134 children under the age of four (that's the age range that children are most at risk for choking on food) died of suffocation in 2011. That's .0000556 percent of all children in this age range. To put that rather hard to fathom fraction in perspective: Your child is four times more likely to be struck by lightning (.0002 percent) than choke on his food. And not all of those asphyxiation deaths were caused by food. In fact, according to the CDC data, only 25 percent were caused by food being lodged in the airway. The other 75 percent of deaths were the result of accidental hangings, choking on non-food items, suffocating on bed sheets or unspecified problems with breathing. While the death of any child is tragic, we need some perspective: Choking deaths among children are rare, and choking deaths caused by food are even more rare.

Where Is Common Sense?

Yet, this reassuring data hasn't stopped the AAP demanding food manufactures add warning labels and "redesign" certain food items, such as hot dogs, so the size, shape and texture make them less likely to lodge in a child's throat. Janet Riley, president of the National Hot Dog and Sausage Council (uh, yes, this organization actually exists), injected a little bit of common sense into the great "hot dog reshape" debate saying:

> As a mother who has fed toddlers cylindrical foods like grapes, bananas, hot dogs and carrots, I 'redesigned' them in my kitchen by cutting them with a paring knife until my children were old enough to manage on their own.

But relying on a parent's common sense simply isn't good enough for alarmists like Dr. Gary Smith, the lead author of the AAP statement, who said in a *USA Today* article that "No parents can watch all of their kids 100% of the time. . . . The best way to protect kids is to design these risks out of existence."

He's correct. Parents simply cannot be expected to watch children 100 percent of the time, and this does indeed leave children vulnerable to dangers. Yet, Smith's simplistic solution to "design risks out of existence" is unrealistic and incredibly naive. How will we rid the world of stones? Coins? Marbles? The keys off of the computer keyboard that my industrious two-year-old once pried out to pop in his mouth? Does Dr. Smith suggest we place children in a bubble to keep them safe from every possible environmental danger?

After all, young children face far greater risks than choking. In fact, a far greater cause of injuries among children (0–14) is falling down—a pretty common occurrence among humans learning to walk and run. The CDC estimates that about 2.8 million children go to the emergency rooms each year because they fall down and hurt themselves. In Dr. Smith's supersafe world stairwells would be banned, high surfaces made illegal and common items in a home—like tables and bookshelves—gathered up and destroyed. What else would Dr. Smith like to see "designed out of existence"?

A better solution might be for the AAP to advise parents to look at a food and determine for themselves its choking potential. Perhaps the AAP could remind parents to tell their kids to eat slowly, take smaller bites and chew. Unfortunately, personal responsibility isn't enough for your benevolent government minder who thinks you're an idiot.

Again, common sense isn't the only casualty here. Dr. Smith and his colleagues at the AAP seem not to understand this, but industry will need to spend money—money that could go to job creation, bonuses for employees, or the creation of other, perhaps healthier, products—on redesigning foods to suit their nanny predilections.

Life Is Risky

Of course, we all want to reduce risks for our children. Yet life itself comes with a certain amount of risk and it's the job of competent adults to mitigate life's risks and to teach children to do the same. Learning how to handle life's risks is critical to human development, and it would be a problem if parents failed to teach children how to *assess* risks on their own.

After all, there's no need to advise your child to chew food completely before swallowing if all food is redesigned to prevent choking. You don't need to tell your kid to stop climbing on high spaces if there are no high spaces to climb. If we do away with cars, there's no need to tell the kids to look both ways when you cross the road . . . and on and on. Reasonable people understand that eliminating all risk during childhood isn't possible, and wouldn't even be desirable if it was possible.

Parents want information so that they can make good decisions for themselves and their families. They should reject those who encourage them to worry about everything under the sun (speaking of that scary, dangerous sun . . .). It's not healthy for them, and it's not healthy for children.

Occasionally, parents should even sit back and appreciate how we are all extremely fortunate to be raising our kids in the modern era where common diseases have been eradicated, child death is rare and modern conveniences make our lives not just easier, but a lot more fun. We should protect our children from true dangers, but not get so overwhelmed that we forget to enjoy life. In fact, I would say the destructive alarmist culture is one aspect of the modern world that you really should try to keep away from your family.

> *"It appears that being wealthier doesn't necessarily mean fewer toxins—in fact, habits considered healthy like eating more vegetables and wearing sunblock appeared to increase toxin levels among richer people."*

Both Rich and Poor Communities Are Affected by Toxic Chemical Exposure

Danielle Kurtzleben

Danielle Kurtzleben is a reporter for U.S. News & World Report. *In the following viewpoint, she examines the surprising results of a recent study by researchers at the University of Exeter in the United Kingdom who studied the connection between income levels and toxic chemical levels. Using data from the Centers for Disease Control and Prevention (CDC), the study found both rich and poor Americans had been exposed to high levels of dangerous toxins—but different toxins. The study reveals that lower-income Americans tended to have higher levels of lead, cadmium, antimony, and other chemicals associated with industrial manufacturing, plastics, smoking, and water and air pollu-*

tion. Higher-income Americans tended to have higher levels of mercury, arsenic, thallium, and other chemicals found in fish, homegrown produce, sunscreen, and waterproof fabrics. The study challenged long-held beliefs that poor communities had a much higher risk of toxic chemical exposure.

As you read, consider the following questions:

1. According to a recent study by the University of Exeter in the United Kingdom, what percentage of the eighteen toxins associated with income were more likely to be present in richer Americans than those at the bottom of the socioeconomic spectrum?

2. Why do the authors of the study believe that wealthier Americans are more likely to have higher levels of mercury in their systems?

3. What common product contains the toxin called BP3?

It's a commonly held belief among some in the environmental community that poorer people are subjected to the most polluted and toxic environments. But a new study suggests all Americans, rich and poor, have their share of toxins; where they are on the income ladder simply determines which poisons are in their bodies.

Using data from the Centers for Disease Control [and Prevention], researchers from the U.K.'s University of Exeter studied the associations between U.S. adults' incomes and levels of 179 toxins. The researchers found that, among 18 toxins that appeared to be associated with income, half were more likely to be present in richer Americans than those at the bottom of the socioeconomic spectrum. That outcome came as a surprise to the scientists who conducted the study.

"We expected chemicals to associate with socioeconomic status, but we anticipated that the majority of chemicals would be higher in poorer individuals," says Jessica Tyrrell, one of the study's authors, in an email to *U.S. News [& World Report]*.

Toxic Chemicals and Low-Income Communities

Tyrrell and her team found that poor Americans tended to have higher levels of lead in their systems than their richer counterparts, which could come from a wide variety of factors, including the air and water, as well as low-income jobs, which are more likely to be industrial and expose workers to lead. Lower-income Americans were also likely to have higher levels of cadmium, potentially a result of smoking, diet, or working in industries like construction and manufacturing. Other toxins more likely to show up among this population were antimony, a metal that people might pick up via smoking or at work, and several toxins found in plastics.

Toxic Chemicals and High-Income Communities

Yet it appears that being wealthier doesn't necessarily mean fewer toxins—in fact, habits considered healthy, like eating more vegetables and wearing sunblock, appeared to increase toxin levels among richer people.

Wealthier Americans are more likely to have mercury and arsenic in their systems, which the authors said may be attributable to fish and shellfish consumption, though dental fillings may also have led to higher mercury levels. They also found that richer people tend to have higher levels of caesium and thallium, which are associated with homegrown produce. They also have higher levels of PFCs [perfluorinated compounds], compounds people might pick up via waterproof fabrics, as well as fresh meat, fish, and other fresh vegetables. Higher-income people, the researchers noted, are more likely to both grow produce and eat those foods. In addition,

"IT'S NOT THE HEAT OR THE HUMIDITY. IT'S THE SULFUR DIOXIDE, HYDROGEN SULFIDE, NON-METHANE HYDROCARBONS AND SULFURIC ACID MIST."

© S. Harris/CartoonStock.com.

wealthier people had higher levels of a toxin called BP3 [benzophenone-3] that is found in sunscreens.

Reevaluating the Threat

This may mean rethinking long-held beliefs about who needs to worry about the health effects of their environment, says Tyrrell.

"Our results suggest that regardless of socioeconomic status, chemicals accumulate in the body. . . . Therefore, in the case of chemical burden, everyone needs to be considered, not just those living in poverty," she says.

Despite these results, special attention will still need to be paid to low-income communities, says one expert.

"Nobody is saying that everyone else isn't exposed to chemicals. We all know that," says Albert Huang, a senior attorney at the Natural Resources Defense Council who specializes in environmental justice.

However, he adds that lower-income communities may have a tougher time escaping those toxins. He says everyday products, like foods and cosmetics, are likely to affect a wide swath of society, but higher-income people are generally less likely to work or live in areas where toxin-heavy industries like chemical refining are prevalent. While it's tough to change one's surroundings, avoiding toxic products is easier with a bit more money, he adds, as more expensive versions of products like sunscreen or cosmetics that contain fewer toxins are available.

"There's everyday products which we're all striving to eliminate from commerce so people, no one gets exposed to them, but then there are industrial toxic exposures on top of that that vulnerable communities are exposed to, especially communities of color and low income," he says.

> "*Low-income parents might not have access to organic produce or be able to guarantee their children a low-lead household. When it comes to brain development, this puts low-income kids at even greater disadvantages—in their education, in their earnings, in their lifelong health and well-being.*"

Toxic Chemical Exposure Disproportionately Impacts Low-Income Communities

James Hamblin

James Hamblin is a senior editor at the Atlantic. *In the following viewpoint, he discusses a 2012 paper published by the National Institutes of Health that identifies a dozen chemicals, including lead, mercury, and organophosphate pesticides, responsible for widespread and cognitive problems in American children. According to researchers, these chemicals have resulted in the loss of forty-one million IQ points and show that there is a "silent pandemic" of damage to the brains of unborn children. Hamblin points out that the risk is even higher in low-income communities because low-income families do not have the financial resources to avoid toxic exposure or to move to areas with lower risk factors.*

As you read, consider the following questions:

1. According to Dr. Philippe Grandjean, how many organophosphate pesticides are there on the US market?

2. How many US senators introduced the Chemical Safety Improvement Act in May 2013?

3. According to economist Elise Gold, how much will lead exposure cost in total income loss for the US population that was six years old or younger in 2006?

Forty-one million IQ points. That's what Dr. David Bellinger determined Americans have collectively forfeited as a result of exposure to lead, mercury, and organophosphate pesticides. In a 2012 paper published by the National Institutes of Health, Bellinger, a professor of neurology at Harvard Medical School, compared intelligence quotients among children whose mothers had been exposed to these neurotoxins while pregnant to those who had not. Bellinger calculates a total loss of 16.9 million IQ points due to exposure to organophosphates, the most common pesticides used in agriculture.

Last month [February 2014], more research brought concerns about chemical exposure and brain health to a heightened pitch. Philippe Grandjean, Bellinger's Harvard colleague, and Philip Landrigan, dean for global health at Mount Sinai School of Medicine [also knonw as the Icahn School of Medicine at Mount Sinai] in Manhattan, announced to some controversy in the pages of a prestigious medical journal that a "silent pandemic" of toxins has been damaging the brains of unborn children. The experts named 12 chemicals—substances found in both the environment and everyday items like furniture and clothing—that they believed to be causing not just lower IQs but ADHD [attention deficit hyperactivity disorder] and autism spectrum disorder. Pesticides were among the toxins they identified.

"So you recommend that pregnant women eat organic produce?" I asked Grandjean, a Danish-born researcher who travels around the world studying delayed effects of chemical exposure on children.

"That's what I advise people who ask me, yes. It's the best way of preventing exposure to pesticides." Grandjean estimates that there are about 45 organophosphate pesticides on the market, and "most have the potential to damage a developing nervous system."

Landrigan had issued that same warning, unprompted, when I spoke to him the week before. "I advise pregnant women to try to eat organic because it reduces their exposure by 80 or 90 percent," he told me. "These are the chemicals I really worry about in terms of American kids, the organophosphate pesticides like chlorpyrifos."

Chlorpyrifos

For decades, chlorpyrifos, marketed by Dow Chemical beginning in 1965, was the most widely used insect killer in American homes. Then, in 1995, Dow was fined $732,000 by the EPA [Environmental Protection Agency] for concealing more than 200 reports of poisoning related to chlorpyrifos. It paid the fine and, in 2000, withdrew chlorpyrifos from household products. Today, chlorpyrifos is classified as "very highly toxic" to birds and freshwater fish, and "moderately toxic" to mammals, but it is still used widely in agriculture on food and non-food crops, in greenhouses and plant nurseries, on wood products and golf courses.

Landrigan has the credentials of some superhero vigilante Doctor America: a Harvard-educated pediatrician, a decorated retired captain of the U.S. Naval Reserve, and a leading physician-advocate for children's health as it relates to the environment. After September 11 [referring to the September 11, 2001, terrorist attacks on the United States], he made news when he testified before Congress in disagreement with the EPA's assessment that asbestos particles stirred into clouds of debris were too small to pose any real threat. Landrigan cited research from mining townships (including Asbestos, Quebec) and argued that even the smallest airborne asbestos fibers could penetrate deeply into a child's lungs.

Double the Risk

Chlorpyrifos is just one of 12 toxic chemicals Landrigan and Grandjean say are having grim effects on fetal brain development. Their new study is similar to a review the two researchers published in 2006, in the same journal, identifying six developmental neurotoxins. Only now they describe twice the danger: The number of chemicals that they deemed to be developmental neurotoxins had doubled over the past seven years. Six had become 12. Their sense of urgency now approached panic. "Our very great concern," Grandjean and Landrigan wrote, "is that children worldwide are being exposed to unrecognized toxic chemicals that are silently eroding intelligence, disrupting behaviors, truncating future achievements and damaging societies."

The chemicals they called out as developmental neurotoxins in 2006 were methylmercury, polychlorinated biphenyls, ethanol, lead, arsenic, and toluene. The additional chemicals they've since found to be toxins to the developing brains of fetuses—and I hope you'll trust me that these all are indeed words—are manganese, fluoride, chlorpyrifos, tetrachloroethylene, polybrominated diphenyl ethers, and dichlorodiphenyltrichloroethane [DDT].

Grandjean and Landrigan note in their research that rates of diagnosis of autism spectrum disorder and ADHD are increasing, and that neurobehavioral development disorders currently affect 10 to 15 percent of births. They add that "subclinical decrements in brain function"—problems with thinking that aren't quite a diagnosis in themselves—"are even more common than these neurobehavioral development disorders."

In perhaps their most salient paragraph, the researchers say that genetic factors account for no more than 30 to 40 percent of all cases of brain development disorders:

> Thus, non-genetic, environmental exposures are involved in causation, in some cases probably by interacting with genetically inherited predispositions. Strong evidence exists that industrial chemicals widely disseminated in the environment are important contributors to what we have called the global, silent pandemic of neurodevelopmental toxicity.

Silent Pandemic

Silent pandemic. When public health experts use that phrase—a relative and subjective one, to be deployed with discretion—they mean for it to echo.

When their paper went to press in the journal the *Lancet Neurology*, the media responded with understandable alarm:

> "A 'Silent Pandemic' of Toxic Chemicals Is Damaging Our Children's Brains, Experts Claim"—*Minneapolis Post*, 2/17/14

> "Researchers Warn of Chemical Impacts on Children,"—*USA Today*, 2/14/14

> "Study Finds Toxic Chemicals Linked to Autism, ADHD"—*Sydney Morning Herald*, 2/16/14

When I first saw these headlines, I was skeptical. It wasn't news that many of the chemicals on this list (arsenic, DDT, lead) are toxic. With each of these substances, the question is just how much exposure does it take to cause real damage. For instance, organophosphates aren't something that anyone would categorically consider safe, in that they are poison. They kill insects by the same mechanism that sarin gas kills people, causing nerves to fire uncontrollably. But like asbestos, they are still legally used in U.S. commerce, with the idea that small amounts of exposure are safe. The adage "the dose makes the poison" may be the most basic premise of toxicology. And hadn't we already taken care of lead? Didn't we already know that alcohol is bad for fetuses? Wasn't fluoride good for teeth?

I found that the real issue was not this particular group of 12 chemicals. Most of them are already being heavily restricted. This dozen is meant to illuminate something bigger: a broken system that allows industrial chemicals to be used without any significant testing for safety. The greater concern lies in what we're exposed to and don't yet know to be toxic. Federal health officials, prominent academics, and even many leaders in the chemical industry agree that the U.S. chemical safety testing system is in dire need of modernization. Yet parties on various sides cannot agree on the specifics of how to change the system, and two bills to modernize testing requirements are languishing in Congress. Landrigan and Grandjean's real message is big, and it involves billion-dollar corporations and Capitol Hill, but it begins and ends with the human brain in its earliest, most vulnerable stages.

Don't Panic?

"When you use the word *pandemic*, that's a scare word," said Laura Plunkett. "And that's my problem. There's a more responsible way to express it. I understand that they want to bring it to attention, but when you bring it to attention, you can still do it in what I would say is a scientifically defensible manner."

Plunkett has a PhD in pharmacology and toxicology. Reviewing articles written in the wake of the publicity around the *Lancet Neurology* paper, I was struck by the definitive title of her blog post on a site called *Science 2.0*: "There Is No Pan-

Meet the Neurotoxins

Manganese   Fluoride   Chlorpyrifos

DDT/DDE   Tetrachloroethylene (PERC)   Polybrominated Diphenyl Ethers (PBDEs)

Arsenic   Lead   Mercury

Toluene   Ethanol   Polychlorinated Biphenyls (PCBs)

TAKEN FROM: James Hamblin, "The Toxins That Threaten Our Brains," *Atlantic*, March 18, 2014.

demic of Chemicals Causing Brain Disorders in Children." Plunkett has been a diplomat for the American Board of Toxicology since 1984. She taught for a while and did research at

NIH, but she is now an independent consultant running her own company, Integrative Biostrategies.

One of her clients is the American Chemistry Council. She also has clients in the food, pesticide, and chemical business—"industry ties," as they say. With that in mind, I sought her out as an established scientist who has worked on the side of the chemical-producing companies. Her blog post about the *Lancet* article was the only response I found telling people not to panic.

"What [Landrigan and Grandjean] are doing with the data is missing the key component, which is the dose," Plunkett explained. "Many of the chemicals they talk about are well established to be neurodevelopmental toxicants in children—but it's all about how much they're exposed to. Just like anything else. If you don't give people enough, or if you don't take enough in your water or food or the air you breathe, you're not going to have an effect."

Plunkett insists that, unlike lead, some of the chemicals on the *Lancet Neurology* list are only developmental toxicants at very high levels—the sort, she says, "that nobody would be exposed to on a daily basis."

Plunkett says she has no problem with a call to ensure that chemical testing is as thorough as possible. "But then to say, and by the way, if you look at the data, 'We've been poisoning people for the last 10 years'? That's a whole other step that isn't supported by the data they point to."

I asked her how concerned American parents should be about certain individual chemicals on Grandjean and Landrigan's list. "I mean, we knew lead was a problem 30 years ago," she said, "and that's why we removed it from gasoline, and that's why we don't let it in solder and cans, and we've taken lead-based paint off the market."

"If you really look at the data on fluoride," she continued, "trying to link an IQ deficit in a population with that chemical is almost impossible to do. Even though statistically, randomly they may have found a relationship, that doesn't prove anything—it identifies a hazard but doesn't prove there's a cause and effect between the two things."

The Problem with Pesticides

What about the chemical that most concerned Landrigan, the pesticide chlorpyrifos?

"No, because the organophosphate pesticides are one of the most highly regulated groups of chemicals that are out there. The EPA regulates those such that if they're used in agriculture, people are exposed to very, very low levels."

Pesticides are indeed more regulated than other industrial chemicals. Before manufacturers can sell pesticides in the U.S., the EPA must ensure that they meet federal standards to protect human health and the environment. Only then will the EPA grant a "registration" or license that permits a pesticide's distribution, sale, and use. The EPA also sets maximum levels for the residue that remains in or on foods once they're sold.

An EPA spokesperson told me that a company introducing a new pesticide must "demonstrate more than 100 different scientific studies and tests from applicants." The EPA also said that since 1996's Food Quality Protection Act, it has added "an additional safety factor to account for developmental risks and incomplete data when considering a pesticide's effect on infants and children, and any special sensitivity and exposure to pesticide chemicals that infants and children may have." Landrigan and Grandjean don't believe that's always sufficient; the dose may make the poison, but not everyone believes the EPA's limits are right for everyone.

When I asked Plunkett whether new industrial chemicals were being screened rigorously enough, even she cited the need to strengthen the Toxic Substances Control Act [TSCA] of 1976. "I'm a very strong proponent of fixing the holes we have," she said, "and we do have some holes under the old system, under TSCA, and those are what the new improvements are going to take care of. They're going to allow us to look at the chemicals out there we don't have a lot of data on—and really those are the ones I'm more concerned about."

The High Price of Lost IQ

Everyone I spoke to for this story agreed that TSCA needs to be fixed. But every attempt has met with bitter opposition. All parties want it to happen; they just want it to happen on their own terms. Unless it does, they don't want it to happen at all.

Last May, a bipartisan group of 22 senators, led by Frank Lautenberg and David Vitter, introduced the Chemical Safety Improvement Act of 2013. Lautenberg, then 89 years old, was the last surviving World War II veteran in the Senate and a longtime champion of environmental safety. (Among other things, he wrote the bill that banned smoking on commercial airlines.) A month after he introduced his TSCA reform bill, Lautenberg died of pneumonia.

After Lautenberg's death, Senator Barbara Boxer told reporters the bill "would not have a chance" of passing without major changes. "I will be honest with you," said Boxer, who chairs the Committee on Environment and Public Works, "this is the most opposition I've ever seen to any bill introduced in this committee." Some of the resistance came from environmental and health advocates who felt the bill would actually make it harder for states to regulate the chemicals that were grandfathered in by TSCA. Their fears intensified in January, after 10,000 gallons of a coal-processing substance poured into West Virginia's Elk River, contaminating a nearby water treatment plant. (The *Wall Street Journal* reported, "Little is known about the chemical's long-term health effects on people, although it isn't believed to be highly toxic.")

The Chemicals in Commerce Act

In February, with Lautenberg's bill stalled in the Senate committee, Republican representative John Shimkus seized the opportunity to introduce another reform option called the

Chemicals in Commerce Act. The chemical industry applauded Shimkus' bill—it won support from the American Chemistry Council, American Cleaning Institute, and the Society of Chemical Manufacturers and Affiliates. Earlier this month at the GlobalChem conference in Baltimore, Dow Chemical's director of products sustainability and compliance Connie Deford said that TCSA reform was in the interests of the chemical sector, acknowledging that consumer confidence in the industry is at an all-time low.

Yet the Chemicals in Commerce Act has provoked strong criticism from groups like the Center for Environmental Health and the Natural Resources Defense Council. A senior scientist with the Environmental Defense Fund called the bill "even more onerous and paralyzing" than the present law, and Representative Henry Waxman, ranking member of the House Energy and Commerce Committee, said the bill "would weaken current law and endanger public health."

The Environmental Protection Agency

I asked the EPA to comment on Landrigan and Grandjean's claim that we are in the midst of a "silent pandemic" and inquired what, if anything, is being done about it. The agency responded by sending me a statement: "EPA has taken action on a number of the chemicals highlighted in this report which have and are resulting in reduced exposures, better understanding, and more informed decisions." The agency included a list of the actions it has already taken to reduce exposure to the chemicals identified in the report. And it emphasized a 2012 "Work Plan," which includes plans to assess more than 80 industrial chemicals in the coming years.

When I emailed the statement to Landrigan, he replied, "Many of the items that they list here are things that I helped to put in place." (In 1997, he spent a sabbatical year setting up EPA's Office of Children's Health Protection.) He agreed that the EPA is doing a lot to protect children from environmental threats. "But the problem is that the good people within EPA are absolutely hamstrung by the lack of strong legislation," he wrote. "They can set up research centers to study chemicals and outreach and education programs, but without strong and enforceable chemical safety legislation, they cannot require industry to test new chemicals before they come to market, and they cannot do recalls of bad chemicals that are already on the market."

Meanwhile, researchers like David Bellinger, who calculated IQ losses, are highlighting the financial cost to society of widespread cognitive decline. Economist Elise Gould has calculated that a loss of one IQ point corresponds to a loss of $17,815 in lifetime earnings. Based on that figure, she estimates that for the population that was six years old or younger in 2006, lead exposure will result in a total income loss of between $165 and $233 billion. The combined current levels of pesticides, mercury, and lead cause IQ losses amounting to around $120 billion annually—or about three percent of the annual budget of the U.S. government.

The Impact on Low-Income Families

Low-income families are hit the hardest. No parent can avoid these toxins—they're in our couches and in our air. They can't be sweated out through hot yoga classes or cleansed with a juice fast. But to whatever extent these things *can* be avoided without better regulations, it costs money. Low-income parents might not have access to organic produce or be able to guarantee their children a low-lead household. When it comes to brain development, this puts low-income kids at even greater disadvantages—in their education, in their earnings, in their lifelong health and well-being.

Grandjean compares the problem to climate change. "We don't have the luxury to sit back and wait until science figures out what's really going on, what the mechanisms are, what the doses are, and that sort of thing. We've seen with lead and mercury and other poisons that it takes decades. And during that time we are essentially exposing the next generation to exactly the kind of chemicals that we want to protect them from."

Periodical and Internet Sources Bibliography

The following articles have been selected to supplement the diverse views presented in this chapter.

Brian Bienkowski and Environmental Health News — "Unregulated Chemicals Found in Drinking Water," *Scientific American*, December 5, 2013.

James Bruggers — "Poor, Minorities Most at Risk from Chemical Stockpiles," *Courier-Journal* (Louisville, KY), May 1, 2014.

Jennifer Canvasser — "Your Life Is the Lab: Toxic Chemicals in 5 Unexpected Places," *Huffington Post*, April 14, 2014.

Deirdre Imus — "Pass It On: The Lasting Danger of Toxic Chemicals," Fox News, December 2, 2013.

Jaeah Lee — "Map: Is There a Risky Chemical Plant Near You?," *Mother Jones*, April 17, 2014.

Renee Lewis and Wilson Dizard — "Report: America's Poorest Minorities at Highest Risk of Chemical Accidents," Al Jazeera America, May 1, 2014.

Lynne Peeples — "More Toxic Chemicals Damaging Children's Brains, New Study Warns," *Huffington Post*, February 14, 2014.

Julia Rogers — "Wristband Detects Wearer's Chemical Exposure," *Portland Tribune* (Oregon), March 31, 2014.

Caroline Snyder — "Biosolids May Contain Toxic Chemicals, Superbugs," *Standard-Examiner* (Ogden, UT), April 25, 2014.

Alice G. Walton — "11 Toxic Chemicals Affecting Brain Development in Children," *Forbes*, February 15, 2014.

OPPOSING
VIEWPOINTS®
SERIES

CHAPTER 2

What Can Lead to Dangerous Levels of Toxic Chemical Exposure?

Chapter Preface

On April 24, 2014, the US Food and Drug Administration (FDA) announced its intention to regulate a wide range of tobacco products, including nicotine gels, cigars, hookah tobacco, and electronic cigarettes, widely known as e-cigarettes. The FDA's move was broadly regarded as controversial because it was viewed as a key step in the federal government's effort to regulate the e-cigarette, which has emerged as a popular alternative to traditional cigarettes. In 2012 e-cigarette sales surpassed 3.5 million, up from just fifty thousand in 2008. If trends continue, it is widely believed that the popularity of e-cigarettes will outpace that of traditional cigarettes within a decade.

Much of that burgeoning popularity stems from the belief that e-cigarettes are a much safer product. E-cigarettes are battery-powered devices fitted with cartridges containing liquid solutions of varying amounts of nicotine, flavorings, and other chemicals. When an individual puffs on the device, known as a vaporizer, it heats the cartridge and emits a vapor, instead of carcinogenic smoke, that is then inhaled. E-cigarettes do not contain tar or other toxic chemicals proven to be a public health risk. Compared to traditional cigarettes, which are blamed for more than four hundred thousand deaths every year, e-cigarettes seem like a cleaner and safer option.

For many in the public health community, however, this is a dangerous misconception. The long-term health effects of inhaling the chemicals found in e-cigarettes—propylene glycol and glycerin food additives—are unknown. There are growing reports of adverse effects from e-cigarette use, including headaches, eye irritation, and coughing. Public health authorities are pushing for more studies of the product's long-term health impacts.

Another safety concern many experts have is the rising rates of e-cigarette use among US teenagers. According to the Centers for Disease Control and Prevention (CDC), e-cigarette use among US high school students and middle schoolers doubled from 2011 to 2012. That dramatic jump has led to concerns that e-cigarettes—which often offer flavors such as cherry, chocolate, vanilla, and cola—could hook young people on nicotine and lead them to become addicted to traditional cigarettes.

That is certainly a concern for Dr. Tom Frieden, the director of the CDC. "I've treated so many adults who are desperate—desperate—to get off tobacco," he told the *Los Angeles Times*. "They all started as kids. I see the industry getting another generation of our kids addicted. To me, as a physician, when 1.78 million of our high school kids have tried an e-cigarette and a lot of them are using it regularly . . . that's like watching someone harm hundreds of thousands of children."

A key benefit of e-cigarettes, defenders argue, is that the product helps chronic smokers kick the habit and can be a potent weapon in the war against tobacco. According to a 2013 survey published in the *American Journal of Preventive Medicine*, about 85 percent of e-cigarette users reported that one of the reasons they started vaping, or using e-cigarettes, was to quit smoking. However, the study did not find strong evidence that e-cigarettes were particularly effective as a smoking-cessation device.

In 2014 the FDA began a long-term study tracking about sixty thousand smokers and nonsmokers to analyze the use of e-cigarettes. Brian King, an epidemiologist at the CDC, maintains that this much-anticipated study will "tell us if people are using them for cessation, or as a gateway to traditional tobacco use."

The debate over the health risks of e-cigarettes is one of the topics explored in the following chapter, which considers factors that could lead to high levels of toxic chemical exposure. Other viewpoints in the chapter consider the health risks from cosmetics, the danger posed by flame-retardant chemicals, and the growing threat from pharmaceutical drugs to the nation's water supply.

| *"The potential for e-cigarettes to help people quit smoking is encouraging."*

E-Cigarettes May Benefit Smokers and Public Health

Sally Satel

Sally Satel is a psychiatrist and a resident scholar at the American Enterprise Institute. In the following viewpoint, she suggests that e-cigarettes could benefit the American public by helping millions of people to stop smoking, saving an estimated half million lives every year. To that end, authorities should encourage smokers to use e-cigarettes by not taxing the product and by allowing vaping in adult environments such as bars, restaurants, and workplaces. Satel acknowledges concerns about e-cigarettes and young people, but she notes that teenage smoking rates are at record lows. In her opinion, e-cigarettes show encouraging promise in reducing smoking rates all over the country and could lead to significant health care savings and other costs.

As you read, consider the following questions:

1. According to Satel, e-cigarettes can help cut the US smoking rate to what by 2020?

2. According to a report from the Centers for Disease Control and Prevention (CDC), how many US middle and high school students have tried e-cigarettes?

3. How much does Satel estimate the direct medical cost of smoking to be per year?

Should electronic cigarettes be regulated like tobacco products, emblazoned with warnings and subject to tight marketing restrictions? Those are among the questions before the Food and Drug Administration [FDA] as it decides in the coming weeks how to handle the battery-powered cigarette mimics that have become a $1.5 billion business in the United States.

Groups promoting intensive regulation include the American Lung Association and the Campaign for Tobacco-Free Kids. They worry that the health risks haven't been fully established and that e-cigarettes will make smoking commonplace again, especially among teens. They are quick to push back in response to anything that might make e-cigarettes more attractive, such as the NJOY King ad that aired during the Super Bowl or when actors Leonardo DiCaprio and Julia Louis-Dreyfus were shown "vaping" at the Golden Globes.

A surgeon general's report released last month [January 2014], on the 50th anniversary of the office's first warning about the dangers of smoking, had little to say about e-cigarettes. Its suggestions for further reducing tobacco use were familiar, including: increase taxes on cigarettes, prohibit indoor smoking, launch media campaigns and reduce the nicotine content of cigarettes.

The Health Benefits of E-Cigarettes

E-cigarettes, however, could be what we need to knock the U.S. smoking rate from a stubborn 18 percent to the government's goal of 12 percent by 2020. We should not only tolerate them but encourage their use.

Although critics stress the need for more research, we can say with high confidence that e-cigarettes are far safer than smoking. No tobacco leaves are combusted, so they don't release the tars and gases that lead to cancer and other smoking-related diseases. Instead, a heating element converts a liquid solution into an aerosol that users exhale as a white plume.

The solution comes in varying concentrations of nicotine—from high (36 mg per milliliter of liquid) to zero—to help people wean themselves off cigarettes, as well as e-cigarettes, and the addictive stimulant in them. But even if people continue using electronic cigarettes with some nicotine, regular exposure has generally benign effects in healthy people, and the FDA has approved the extended use of nicotine gums, patches and lozenges.

The other main ingredients in e-cigarettes are propylene glycol and glycerin. These are generally regarded as harmless—they're found in toothpaste, hand sanitizer, asthma inhalers, and many other FDA-approved foods, cosmetics and pharmaceuticals. There are also traces of nitrosamines, known carcinogens, but they are present at levels comparable to the patch and at far lower concentrations than in regular cigarettes—500- to 1,400-fold lower. Cadmium, lead and nickel may be there, too, but in amounts and forms considered nontoxic.

"Few, if any, chemicals at levels detected in electronic cigarettes raise serious health concerns," a 2011 study in the *Journal of Public Health Policy* determined. "A preponderance of the available evidence shows [e-cigarettes] to be much safer than tobacco cigarettes and comparable in toxicity to conventional nicotine replacement products."

Encouraging Potential

The potential for e-cigarettes to help people quit smoking is encouraging. Yet so far there has been little research on their effectiveness. A study published in the *Lancet* in November

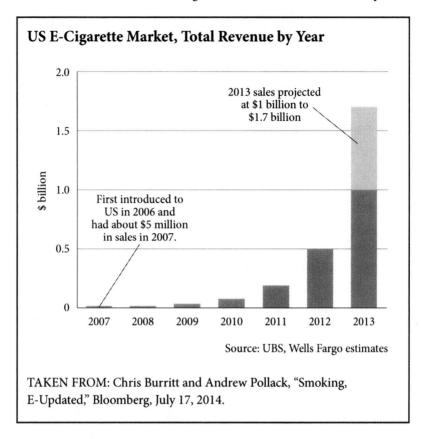

US E-Cigarette Market, Total Revenue by Year

2013 sales projected at $1 billion to $1.7 billion

First introduced to US in 2006 and had about $5 million in sales in 2007.

Source: UBS, Wells Fargo estimates

TAKEN FROM: Chris Burritt and Andrew Pollack, "Smoking, E-Updated," Bloomberg, July 17, 2014.

concluded that e-cigarettes, with or without nicotine, were as effective as nicotine patches for helping smokers quit. Granted, patches have had a disappointing record in helping people stay off cigarettes for more than a few months. But there are reasons to think that e-cigarettes would be even more effective outside the laboratory.

Participants in the *Lancet* study were randomly assigned to nicotine e-cigarettes, patches or placebo e-cigarettes. In the real world, of course, people get to choose. And e-cigarettes have several advantages over patches and gums. For one, they provide a quicker fix, because the pulmonary route is the fastest practical way to deliver nicotine to the brain. They also offer visual, tactile and gestural similarities to traditional cigarettes.

Reporter Megan McArdle tested the comparison for a *Bloomberg Businessweek* article this month: "After I'd put it together, I had something surprisingly close to one of the cigarettes I used to smoke. The mentholated tobacco flavor rolled sinuously over my tongue, hit the back of my throat in an unctuously familiar cloud, and rushed through my capillaries, buzzing along my dormant nicotine receptors. The only thing missing was the unpleasant clawing feeling in my chest as my lungs begged me not to pollute them with tar and soot."

Concerns

This is where antismoking advocates get worried about e-cigarettes being too attractive and encouraging people—especially young people—to become addicted to nicotine and, in some cases, to progress to smoking. The Centers for Disease Control and Prevention [CDC] stoked concerns with data released in September showing that 1.78 million middle and high school students had tried e-cigarettes and that one in five middle school students who reported trying them said they hadn't tried traditional cigarettes. "This raises concern that there may be young people for whom e-cigarettes could be an entry point to use of conventional tobacco products, including cigarettes," the CDC concluded.

According to that same CDC study, however, an extremely small percentage of teenagers use e-cigarettes regularly—only 2.8 percent of high school students reported using one in the previous 30 days in 2012. And while that number is rising—it was 1.5 percent in 2011—teenage cigarette smoking rates are at record lows. That might suggest that increased exposure to e-cigarettes isn't encouraging more people to smoke. But the numbers are so small that it's too early to make definitive claims about the relationship between teen vaping and smoking.

More Research

Yes, we still need research on the long-term health and behavioral impacts of e-cigarettes. Brad Rodu, a pathologist at the University of Louisville, offers an apt analogy between electronic cigarettes and cell phones. When cell phones became popular in the late '90s, there were no data on their long-term safety. As it turns out, the risk of a brain tumor with prolonged cell phone use is not zero, but it is very small and of uncertain health significance.

In the case of e-cigarettes, Rodu says that "at least a decade of continued use by thousands of users would need to transpire before confident assessments could be conducted." Were the FDA to ban e-cigarette marketing until then, the promise of vaping would be put on hold. Meanwhile, millions of smokers who might otherwise switch would keep buying tobacco products. "We can't say that decades of e-cigarette use will be perfectly safe," Rodu told me, "but for cigarette users, we are sure that smoke is thousands of times worse."

Recommendations

The FDA should call for reliable, informative labeling and safe manufacturing standards for e-cigarettes. It should also allay concerns about potential gateway use and youth addiction to nicotine by banning the marketing and sale of e-cigarettes to minors. It should not be heavy-handed in restricting marketing and sales to adults.

Instead, promoting electronic cigarettes to smokers should be a public health priority. Given that the direct medical costs of smoking are estimated to be more than $130 billion per year, along with $150 billion annually in productivity losses from premature deaths, getting more smokers to switch would result in significant cost savings—as well as almost half a million lives saved each year.

We should make e-cigarettes accessible to smokers by eschewing hefty taxes, if we tax them at all, and offering free samples and starter kits. Those kits, which contain a battery, a charger and nicotine-liquid cartridges, typically run between $30 and $90. To reduce the hurdle to initiation, any payer of smoking-related costs—health insurers, [Department of] Veterans Affairs medical centers, companies that offer smoking-cessation programs for their employees, Medicare, Medicaid—should make the starter kits available gratis. Users should have to pay for their own replacement cartridges, but those are much cheaper than cigarette packs.

Also, we should allow and welcome public vaping in adult environments such as bars, restaurants and workplaces. Vapers would serve as visual prompts for smokers to ask about vaping and, ideally, ditch traditional cigarettes and take up electronic ones instead.

It may be hard for antismoking activists to feel at ease with e-cigarettes in light of their view that traditional cigarette makers have long downplayed the health dangers of their product. This perception has generated distrust of anything remotely resembling the act of smoking. It doesn't help that major tobacco companies are now investing in e-cigarettes.

But if we embrace electronic cigarettes as a way for smokers to either kick their nicotine addictions or, at least, obtain nicotine in a safer way, they could help instigate the wave of smoking cessation that antismoking activists—and all of us—are hoping for.

> *"Acting on growing evidence that these flame retardants can accumulate in people and cause adverse health effects—interfering with hormones, reproductive systems, thyroid and metabolic function, and neurological development in infants and children— the federal government and various states have limited or banned the use of some of these chemicals, as have other countries."*

Flame-Retardant Chemicals Are a Public Health Threat

Elizabeth Grossman

Elizabeth Grossman is a journalist and an author. In the following viewpoint, she surveys some of the growing evidence that shows that flame-retardant chemicals are detrimental to human health, especially in fetal and early development. Grossman notes that flame-retardant chemicals are ubiquitous in modern society—found in electronics, upholstery, carpets, textiles, insulation, and children's clothing and strollers. As the realization of the health dangers of flame retardants have been revealed, the fed-

Elizabeth Grossman, "Are Flame Retardants Safe? Growing Evidence Says 'No,'" *Yale Environment 360*, September 29, 2011. Copyright © 2011 Elizabeth Grossman. All rights reserved. Reproduced by permission.

eral government and various states have passed legislation to limit—or even ban—their use. Studies show, however, that despite the ban of certain flame retardants, these dangerous compounds are consistently used in the United States and other countries. Experts recommend that industries alleviate the need for flame retardants by replacing petroleum-based materials in their products with safer, nonflammable ones, despite the challenge in sourcing these products.

As you read, consider the following questions:

1. What is the value of the flame retardants industry, according to the author?

2. According to the American Chemistry Council, halogenated flame retardants prevent how many deaths every year?

3. What company has commissioned the milling of its own patented, organic cotton-wool blend fabrics that are fire resistant, according to Grossman?

Over the past 40 years, a class of chemicals with the tongue-twisting name of halogenated flame retardants has permeated the lives of people throughout the industrialized world. These synthetic chemicals—used in electronics, upholstery, carpets, textiles, insulation, vehicle and airplane parts, children's clothes and strollers, and many other products—have proven very effective at making petroleum-based materials resist fire.

Yet many of these compounds have also turned out to be environmentally mobile and persistent—turning up in food and household dust—and are now so ubiquitous that levels of the chemicals in the blood of North Americans appear to have been doubling every two to five years for the past several decades.

Futile Bans

Acting on growing evidence that these flame retardants can accumulate in people and cause adverse health effects—interfering with hormones, reproductive systems, thyroid and metabolic function, and neurological development in infants and children—the federal government and various states have limited or banned the use of some of these chemicals, as have other countries. Several are restricted by the Stockholm Convention on Persistent Organic Pollutants. Many individual companies have voluntarily discontinued production and use of these compounds. Yet despite these restrictions, evidence has emerged in recent months that efforts to curtail the use of such flame retardants—a $4 billion-a-year industry globally—and to limit their impacts on human health may not be succeeding.

The Danger to Babies and Children

This spring and summer, a test of consumer products, as well as a study in *Environmental Science & Technology*, showed that use of these chemicals continues to be widespread and that compounds thought to be off the market due to health concerns continue to be used in the U.S., including in children's products such as crib mattresses, changing table pads, nursing pillows, and car seats. Also this summer, new research provided the first strong evidence that maternal exposure to a widely used type of flame retardant, known as PBDEs (polybrominated diphenyl ethers), can alter thyroid function in pregnant women and children, result in low birth weights, and impair neurological development.

"Of most concern are developmental and reproductive effects and early life exposures—*in utero*, infantile and for children," Linda Birnbaum, director of the National Institute of Environmental Health Sciences and the National Toxicology Program, said in an interview.

Heather Stapleton, assistant professor of environmental chemistry at Duke University and lead author of the recent *Environmental Science & Technology* study, said more action from industry and government regulators is urgently needed. "My concern is the elevated exposure infants and toddlers are receiving," Stapleton said in an email. "A high proportion of infants are in physical contact with products treated with these chemicals almost 24 hours a day. Some of these chemicals are either known or suspected carcinogens. During the first year of life, infants are still developing, particularly their brain. And some of these flame-retardant chemicals have chemical structures similar to known developmental neurotoxicants (e.g., organophosphate pesticides)."

The Impact on Fetal Development

In one study, published this summer in the *American Journal of Epidemiology*, University of California, Berkeley, researchers found that each tenfold increase in levels of various brominated flame retardants in a mother's blood was associated with an approximately 115 gram decrease in her baby's birth weight, a drop the researchers describe as "relatively large."

"What makes this significant, is that this is the first long study that suggests maternal exposure to PBDEs may impact fetal development and health," explained lead author Kim Harley, associate director for health effects at the University of California, Berkeley, Center for Environmental Research and Children's Health.

Despite Bans, New Products Hit the Market

As evidence linking the use of halogenated flame retardants to health risks continues to mount, there is increasing pressure on government and industry to take action. About a dozen U.S. states have enacted laws that bar certain uses of various flame retardants. Among these regulations are those that bar the use of two or more polybrominated diphenyl ethers (PBDEs), particularly in children's products. New York recently passed a law limiting use of the flame retardant known as Tris, while the European Union limits the use of certain halogenated flame retardants in electronics—a regulation that most companies comply with worldwide. The U.S. Consumer Product Safety Commission barred Tris from children's clothing in 1977 after it was identified as a carcinogen and a mutagen. And using its authority under the Toxic Substances Control Act, the U.S. Environmental Protection Agency (EPA) and PBDE manufacturers have worked out a voluntary phaseout of these compounds that began in 2004 and is to conclude in 2013.

Yet new halogenated flame retardants with chemical compositions and structures similar to those that are now regulated, including PBDEs, continue to enter the market. (This class of compounds typically uses bromine and chlorine, elements known as halogens, to inhibit combustion.) Meanwhile, those that are restricted are being found in products from which they've been barred, most likely due to various flaws in supply-chain oversight. At the same time, older products containing discontinued flame retardants remain in use; many of these products—furniture, carpeting, car seats, and strollers, for example—are designed to last for years, prolonging exposure to chemicals with documented adverse health effects. But tracking the use of individual flame retardants is challenging, as product labels are not required to declare these substances, nor are chemical manufacturers required to reveal full details of what goes into their products.

The American Chemistry Council (ACC) and other chemical industry groups maintain the safety of currently manufactured flame retardants, and the ACC says that in the U.S. each year flame retardants prevent 360 deaths and 740 injuries that would have resulted from furniture fires alone.

The Challenge of Eliminating Flame Retardants

So how can use of these compounds be reduced or eliminated?

The EPA is in the process of assessing potential alternatives to PBDEs and other flame retardants. But a list of potential alternatives released last month includes numerous other halogenated compounds, and many chemicals on the list will likely fail to meet the program's health-safety goals.

Some experts say what is sorely needed is for industry to begin relying less on the highly flammable, petroleum-based materials used in so many consumer products. "It's essential that we rethink the base materials we use to make products," said Kathy Curtis, policy director of Clean [& Healthy] New York, a nonprofit organization advocating for chemical safety. "Styrene insulation is so flammable that flame retardants are required, and they still burn quite easily. Polyurethane foam in furniture and baby care products is also highly flammable, despite the added flame retardants certain flammability standards require. We have to stop using such fuel-rich, petroleum-based materials in buildings when safer, inherently flame-retardant substitutes are available for these same uses."

John Warner, president of the Warner Babcock Institute for Green Chemistry, said that industry has become so reliant on flame retardants that as much as a third of the weight of plastics used in airplanes comes from one type of PBDE flame retardant, known as "deca." Finding an alternative will be challenging, said Warner, especially since from a fire-safety point of view deca is "tried and true," and it is used in so many different types of plastics and foams. There are viable nontoxic alternatives to using halogenated flame retardants, Warner explained, but thus far, not one that will work as a drop-in substitute for all uses of deca.

New Strategies

Two companies that manufacture children's products are working to eliminate the need for flame-retardant chemicals by using fabrics whose density and composition enable them to meet flammability standards without chemical additives. Joseph Hei, president and founder of Orbit Baby, said his company has commissioned the milling of its own patented, organic cotton-wool blend fabrics that are fire resistant. The safety of the products is certified to the Oeko-Tex 100 standard. . . . "We verify and do our own follow-up screening of these fabrics," Hei said in an interview.

Andreas Zandren, vice president for sales, marketing, and product development for BabyBjörn, said his company has found a similar solution by using a densely woven cotton in some products and thinner foams that don't require use of flame retardants. BabyBjörn does in-house testing of all fabrics to make sure they are free of hazardous flame retardants, Zandren said.

Hei explained that there are relatively few mills that offer Oeko-Tex certified fabrics, adding, "It's a sourcing challenge." Both companies also acknowledged that meeting California's tough flammability standards and U.S. car flammability regulations is challenging. But, said Zandren, "Strict standards challenge us to be very creative in sourcing and testing new materials, as well as creating smart designs."

Raising Awareness

This kind of sourcing and testing is costly, as reflected in these companies' product prices when compared with other more mass-market brands. Asked about the relatively high price of Orbit Baby products and what that means for lower-income consumers, Hei said that he hoped awareness would lead to more demand for the kinds of materials his company is using and thus lead to lower prices. Several larger companies, among them Graco and Walmart, make car seats also rated as low in flame retardants by the Michigan-based nonprofit, Healthy Stuff.org. Walmart restricts use of PBDEs in children's and other products, but declined to discuss details of what alternatives their products use to meet safety standards. Graco also declined comment on that issue.

Eventually, product redesign that avoids flammable materials will be key, experts said.

"I think we should be asking, 'Where do we really need them?'" said Linda Birnbaum of the National Institute of Environmental Health Sciences. "I don't question the need for flame retardants in an airplane, but do we need them in nursing pillows and babies' strollers? Are we putting chemicals in places we don't need them?"

> "Reliable figures are hard to come by, but it's a safe assumption that we, as consumers, are responsible for a hefty percentage of the pharmaceutical and personal care products that wind up in lakes, rivers, and streams."

Pharmaceutical Drugs Are Polluting Water and Adversely Affecting Wildlife

Harvard Health Letter

The Harvard Health Letter *is a monthly newsletter published by Harvard Health Publications that focuses on the latest news on health and well-being. In the following viewpoint, the author reports that authorities are increasingly concerned about the impact of chemicals from prescription drugs and over-the-counter medications on our water supply and on aquatic life. The author lists sources of pharmaceutical pollution, including agriculture, drug manufacturing, and inadequate disposal of pharmaceutical drugs. In some cases, chemicals enter the water supply from sweat, excretion or urination, and lotions and creams. Individuals can reduce their pharmaceutical footprint by limiting bulk*

"Drugs in the Water," Excerpted from the *Harvard Health Letter*, June 2011 © 2011; Harvard University. For more information visit: www.health.harvard.edu. Reproduced by permission.

purchases of drugs and utilizing local drug take-back programs, which collect outdated and unused prescription drugs and dispose of them properly.

As you read, consider the following questions:

1. According to the author, how many public water systems around the country monitor for harmful substances?

2. How much does the amount of ibuprofen and naproxen in the water discharged from sewage treatment plants decrease because of conventional treatment methods?

3. What does the author cite as the adverse effects of pharmaceuticals in the water on aquatic life?

Although maybe not as tasty as an ice-cold gulp from a mountain spring, the water that flows through most American kitchen faucets is generally clean, clear, and safe. Approximately 170,000 public water systems are monitored for nearly 80 harmful substances. The prohibited nasties include bacteria, viruses, pesticides, petroleum products, strong acids, and some metals.

But water-quality experts and environmental advocates are increasingly concerned about another kind of water pollution: chemicals from prescription drugs and over-the-counter medications that get into lakes, rivers, and streams. Water also gets contaminated by perfume, cologne, skin lotions, and sunscreens that wash off people's skin.

At this point, there's really no evidence of pharmaceutical and personal care products in the water harming people, but studies are showing adverse effects on aquatic life.

Drug take-back programs, which allow people to drop off their unused medications at central locations, serve two purposes. They keep unused drugs out of the water and prevent diversion of drugs, mainly the opioid painkillers, for recreation and illegal purposes.

Another step in the right direction is new guidelines from the federal Environmental Protection Agency (EPA) that discourage hospitals and nursing homes from flushing unused drugs down the drain or toilet. Guidelines for individuals also discourage flushing most, but not all, unused drugs. The question now is whether these and other efforts will be enough to keep the chemicals out of the water at a time when the use of pharmaceuticals and personal care products continues to grow at a rapid rate.

The Sources

Reliable figures are hard to come by, but it's a safe assumption that we, as consumers, are responsible for a hefty percentage of the pharmaceutical and personal care products that wind up in lakes, rivers, and streams. The typical American medicine cabinet is full of unused and expired drugs, only a fraction of which get disposed of properly. Data collected from a medication collection program in California in 2007 suggest that about half of all medications—both prescription and over-the-counter—are discarded. That's probably a high-end estimate, but even if the real proportion is lower, there's a lot of unused medication that can potentially get into the water.

Chemicals also get into the water from the drugs we use. Our bodies metabolize only a fraction of most drugs we swallow. Most of the remainder is excreted in urine or feces (some is sweated out) and therefore gets into wastewater. An increasing number of medications are applied as creams or lotions, and the unabsorbed portions of those medications can contribute to the pollution problem when they get washed off. It's been calculated, for example, that one man's use of testosterone cream can wind up putting as much of the hormone into the water as the natural excretions from 300 men.

Health care institutions are another source of pharmaceutical water pollution. Hospitals are probably less of a problem than nursing homes because they typically have on-site pharmacies with arrangements in place to return unused drugs to manufacturers for credit or disposal. Nursing homes, though, have often been guilty of flushing medications down the toilet or drain after a patient dies or is transferred to another facility. Typically, they don't have the same kind of return arrangements as hospitals. And the rules for getting rid of opioid painkillers, which make disposal down the drain an acceptable option, have inadvertently encouraged some nursing homes to dispose of all their leftover medications that way.

Drug manufacturing also results in some pharmaceutical pollution, although some factories are bigger problems than others. For example, a U.S. Geological Survey study found contamination levels downstream from two drug manufacturing plants in New York State that were 10 to 1,000 times higher than those at comparable facilities around the country.

Agriculture is another major source. The two trillion pounds of animal waste generated by large-scale poultry and livestock operations in this country is laced with hormones and antibiotics fed to animals to make them grow faster and to keep them from getting sick. Inevitably, some of those hormones and antibiotics leach into groundwater or get into waterways.

How Bad Is the Problem?

A study conducted by the U.S. Geological Survey in 1999 and 2000 found measurable amounts of one or more medications in 80% of the water samples drawn from a network of 139 streams in 30 states. The drugs identified included a witches' brew of antibiotics, antidepressants, blood thinners, heart medications (ACE [angiotensin-converting enzyme] inhibitors, calcium-channel blockers, digoxin), hormones (estrogen, progesterone, testosterone), and painkillers. Scores of studies have been done since. Other drugs that have been found include caffeine (which, of course, comes from many other sources besides medications); carbamazepine, an antiseizure

© Paul Fell/CartoonStock.com.

drug; fibrates, which improve cholesterol levels; and some fragrance chemicals (galaxolide and tonalide).

Sewage treatment plants are not currently designed to remove pharmaceuticals from water. Nor are the facilities that treat water to make it drinkable. Yet a certain amount of pharmaceutical contamination is removed when water gets treated for other purposes. For example, some research shows that conventional treatment methods result in a 90% decrease in the amount of ibuprofen and naproxen in the water discharged from sewage treatment plants. On the other hand, treatment doesn't seem to have much effect on the levels of drugs such as carbamazepine and diclofenac (a pain reliever).

Some aspects of sewage treatment may remove pharmaceuticals from the water, but as a result, concentrations in sludge increase. Some of that sludge is used as fertilizer, so the pharmaceuticals are getting into the environment in another way.

Drinking-water treatment may also get rid of some pharmaceutical contamination. Chlorine is used to kill bacteria and other pathogens, but it also seems to degrade or remove acetaminophen, codeine, and the antibiotic sulfathiazole. A 2007 study of one drinking-water plant found that conventional treatment methods reduced the concentrations of several important medications (acetaminophen, carbamazepine) by 75%.

Still, there's really not much question that some pharmaceutical pollution persists and does wind up in the water we drink. In 2008, the Associated Press published a series of investigative articles about pharmaceutical contamination in drinking water. The journalists uncovered test results that showed the water supplies for 24 major metropolitan areas had detectable levels of pharmaceuticals. Scientists from the Southern Nevada Water Authority and other organizations reported results in 2010 from a study analyzing drinking water from 19 treatment plants. Their tests found antidepressants, antipsychotics, antibiotics, beta blockers, and tranquilizers, although only in trace amounts and far below levels thought to have an effect on humans.

It's possible that there's a cumulative effect on people from even tiny amounts of these and other pharmaceuticals in drinking water, but this hasn't been proven. And perhaps vulnerable populations (pregnant women, people with disabilities) are affected, although that's also unproven.

Effects on Fish and Wildlife

In contrast to the uncertainty about human health effects, there's quite a bit of evidence for pharmaceuticals in the water affecting aquatic life, particularly fish. Numerous studies have shown that estrogen and chemicals that behave like it have a feminizing effect on male fish and can alter female-to-male ratios. Sources of estrogen include birth control pills and postmenopausal hormone treatments, as well as the estrogen that women produce naturally and excrete. Intersex fish—creatures with both male and female sex characteristics—have been found in heavily polluted sections of the Potomac River. Studies of fish upstream and downstream of wastewater treatment plants have found more female and intersex fish downstream from the plants, presumably because of the higher estrogen levels in the downstream water. Other research has uncovered popular antidepressant medications concentrated in the brain tissue of fish downstream from wastewater treatment plants.

4 Ways to Reduce Your Pharmaceutical Footprint

- Limit bulk purchases. Volume discounts make the price attractive, but big bottles of unused pills create an opportunity for medications to end up in the water.

- Use drug take-back programs. A federal law went into effect in 2010 that makes it easier for those programs to be organized at a local level, so you may see one in your community. The federal Drug Enforcement [Administration] has held two national drug take-back days and is likely to organize some more.

- Do not flush unused medicines or pour them down the drain. This is the very least you can do. But the FDA advises that certain powerful narcotic pain medications should be flushed because of concerns about accidental overdose or illicit use unless you can find a drug take-back program that will accept them.

- Be careful about how you throw medications into the trash. Medications thrown into the trash end up being incinerated or buried in landfills, which is preferable to flushing them or pouring them down the drain. If you put them in the trash, remove them from the packaging, crush them, and seal them in a plastic bag with some water. You're supposed to add sawdust, cat litter, coffee grounds, or some other unappealing material to the bag. That isn't for environmental reasons, but to cut down on the chances that a child or animal might eat the contents. You should also be careful to peel off any identifying information from containers of prescription medicine.

Bigger Changes

On a larger scale, the EPA has taken a four-pronged approach that involves public education, stepped-up monitoring of water supplies, partnerships with health care facilities and agribusinesses to reduce waste, and eventually, perhaps, new regulations. As an introductory step toward possible regulation, the EPA has added 10 pharmaceutical compounds—one antibiotic and nine hormones—to its watch list of potentially harmful contaminants that warrant greater investigation.

The Natural Resources Defense Council, an environmental group, has called on drug manufacturers to design "eco-friendly" drugs that are absorbed by the body more efficiently or will break down in the environment after they're excreted. The organization has also asked companies to implement techniques to limit bioactive waste generated in their manufacturing processes.

| "It gets worse: the list of toxic additives present in many cosmetics is jaw-droppingly huge."

Many Common Cosmetics Contain Toxins and May Be a Threat to Public Health

Linda Sharps

Linda Sharps is a writer. In the following viewpoint, she researches the health and environmental impact of the cosmetics, bath products, skin care products, and fragrances that Americans use on a daily basis. Sharps discovers that many of these products contain carcinogens, reproductive toxins, and other harmful chemicals, most of which are absorbed into the skin. Some of these toxins enter the water supply when they are used in the shower or rinsed off at night. She finds it disconcerting that the US Food and Drug Administration (FDA) does not even evaluate the safety of many of the ingredients found in common cosmetics. Sharps recommends a few ways to help consumers evaluate the safety of cosmetics on their own.

As you read, consider the following questions:

1. According to the author, how many cosmetic products does the average person use every day?

Linda Sharps, "Beauty and Its Beastly Secrets: The Toxic Truth About Cosmetics," TakePart, October 29, 2013. This is reprinted with the permission of TakePart, LLC from www.takepart.com. © TakePart, LLC 2013.

2. What percentage of what we put on our skin does the author report gets absorbed into the bloodstream?

3. What will be the value of the cosmetics industry by 2017, according to Sharps?

Would you believe the average person uses up to 15 different cosmetic products a day? It's shocking, when you consider how easy it is to simply drink plenty of water, get a full night's rest, and of course embrace the natural appearance you were born with. Why, I might occasionally apply a little raw coconut oil or press a fresh organic beet against my lips, but otherwise I—

Okay FINE. Right now I'm wearing moisturizer, skin primer, foundation, under-eye concealer, eyeliner, bronzer, blush, eyebrow powder, setting power, and lip stain—and that was just to make myself look halfway human for school drop-off. (At 39, I find that my morning ablutions are less about glamour, and more about not appearing *quite* as seemingly flu-ridden as I looked when I first got out of bed.)

I use a ridiculous amount of different cosmetics products on a regular basis, from skin care items to makeup to fragrance. This is why I thought it would be interesting to tackle the issue of whether or not all these different salves, powders, and snake oils are bad for me or the environment.

The Shocking Truth About Cosmetics

And by "interesting" I mean "completely terrifying." Here are a few facts I discovered almost immediately:

- According to the Environmental Working Group, 89 percent of 10,500 ingredients used in personal care products have not been evaluated for safety by the FDA [US Food and Drug Administration].

How Does the Law Define a Cosmetic?

The Federal Food, Drug, and Cosmetic Act (FD&C Act) defines cosmetics by their intended use, as "articles intended to be rubbed, poured, sprinkled, or sprayed on, introduced into, or otherwise applied to the human body . . . for cleansing, beautifying, promoting attractiveness, or altering the appearance" [FD&C Act, sec. 201(i)]. Among the products included in this definition are skin moisturizers, perfumes, lipsticks, fingernail polishes, eye and facial makeup preparations, cleansing shampoos, permanent waves, hair colors, and deodorants, as well as any substance intended for use as a component of a cosmetic product.

"Is It a Cosmetic, a Drug, or Both? (Or Is It a Soap?),"
FDA.gov, 2014.

- In fact, the US federal government doesn't require any health studies or pre-market testing on personal care products.

- As a result, many cosmetics are thought to contain carcinogens, reproductive toxins, and other chemicals that may pose health risks.

- Up to 60% of what we put on our skin gets absorbed into the bloodstream.

It gets worse: The list of toxic additives present in many cosmetics is jaw-droppingly huge. U.S. researchers report that *one in eight* of the 82,000 ingredients used in personal care products are industrial chemicals. Harmful ingredients in your makeup drawer that should be avoided at all costs include (but are certainly not limited to): butyl acetate, butylated hydroxytoluene, coal tar, cocamide DEA/lauramide DEA, diazolidinyl urea, ethyl acetate, formaldehyde, parabens (methyl, ethyl, propyl and butyl), petrolatum, phthalates, propylene glycol, siloxanes, sodium laureth/sodium lauryl sulfate, talc, toluene, triclosan, and triethanolamine.

The Environmental Impact

Here's where I want to just bury my head in the sand and whine defensively that if I'm applying poison to my skin on a daily basis, am I really hurting anyone other than myself? I mean, it's not like I go outside and dump endocrine disrupters, reproductive toxicants, and neurotoxins directly into the EARTH, right?

Well, no ... but also yes.

Every time I take a shower or bath, I'm washing all those toxins into the water system. Nanoparticles used in sunscreens and cosmetics (found in leading brands like Clinique, Clarins, L'Oréal, Revlon, the Body Shop, Max Factor, and Lancôme Paris) may have incredibly harmful effects on bacteria and a certain type of beneficial soil microbe. Mercury from some cosmetics sold illegally in the U.S. (primarily skin lightening products) can enter the environment in wastewater, and may be transformed there into methylmercury, an even more toxic compound.

It's also believed that chemicals that are commonly used in sunscreen can activate a virus and which threatens coral. Sunscreen! The stuff we all use at the damn beach.

Oh, and as if this all isn't bad enough, there's the small matter of the carbon footprint created by the cosmetics companies, an industry that's projected to reach $265 billion by 2017. We're talking energy and water consumption, emissions to the environment, packaging waste, and more.

Take Action

So what's a beauty product junkie to do in the face of all this depressing news? There's certainly no easy answer, because sifting through the marketing jargon to determine a product's eco-status is harder than you'd think. The FDA doesn't review or regulate this stuff, so words like "natural" or "hypoallergenic" are essentially meaningless.

Thankfully, some organizations have made the process as pain-free as possible. The Environmental Working Group has a Skin Deep online database, where you can instantly check the safety of over 78,000 personal care products. The Compact for Safe Cosmetics has a useful FAQ titled "What Should I Buy?" And there's an iPhone app called "Think Dirty" that allows you to scan the bar code of a cosmetics or personal care product (in the store, before you buy it!), and rates it across three different categories: Carcinogenicity, Developmental & Reproductive Toxicity, and Allergies & Immunotoxicities.

I'll be honest: It was always easier for me to believe that only paranoid tree-hugging types really cared about chemicals in cosmetics. I sort of thought that once you focused on this stuff, it was a slippery slope to morphing into Julianne Moore in *Safe*, claiming violent sensitivities to every synthetic substance on the planet.

I don't feel that way anymore. I'm not quite ready to throw out my existing makeup stash, but I will absolutely be checking labels from here on out. Just like every other environmental effort, even the smallest change has the potential to add up to a big difference.

Do you check makeup labels and avoid certain chemicals?

Periodical and Internet Sources Bibliography

The following articles have been selected to supplement the diverse views presented in this chapter.

Jacqueline Silvestri Banks	"Are Toxic Chemicals Lurking in Your Favorite Beauty Products?," Fox News, April 8, 2014.
Victoria Colliver	"BPA-Free Plastics May Be Less Safe than Those with Chemical," SFGate.com, March 9, 2014.
Dawn Fallik	"This New Study Found More Drugs in Our Drinking Water than Anybody Knew: And No One's Doing Anything About It," *New Republic*, December 11, 2013.
Serena Gordon	"Makeup's Possible Downside: Chemicals, Allergy Triggers, and Other Dangers," *Newsday* (Melville, New York), April 25, 2014.
Deirdre Imus	"Is Your Drinking Water on Drugs?," Fox News, December 18, 2013.
Deborah Kotz	"Boston Health Chief Urges FDA to Be Tougher on E-Cigarettes," *Boston Globe*, May 2, 2014.
Dina Fine Maron	"Smoke Screen: Are E-Cigarettes Safe?," *Scientific American*, May 1, 2014.
Heather Somerville	"Exposure to Harmful Chemicals in Personal Care Products and Household Goods Has Declined, Study Says," *San Jose Mercury News*, January 14, 2014.
Emily Thomas	"Liquid Nicotine in E-Cigarettes Could Be Deadly," *Huffington Post*, March 24, 2014.
Jacque Wilson and Jen Christensen	"7 Other Chemicals in Your Food," CNN, February 10, 2014.

CHAPTER 3

How Are Chemicals Endangering the Water and Food Supply?

Chapter Preface

On August 5, 2005, President George W. Bush signed into law the Energy Policy Act of 2005 at Sandia National Laboratories in Albuquerque, New Mexico. The act covered a broad range of energy policies affecting renewable energies to fossil fuels. For the environmental community, the act was a mixed bag. Some of the policies drew support from environmentalists: for example, the act provided for tax credits for the owners of hybrid vehicles and homeowners who made energy-saving improvements to their homes. It authorized subsidies for wind and other renewable energy sources, which was a boon to the alternative energy industry, and provided support for the geothermal industry.

Yet there was also plenty in the Energy Policy Act to concern environmentalists. It authorized the secretary of the interior to begin the process of evaluating public lands in Colorado, Utah, and Wyoming for commercial leasing to energy companies for oil shale and tar sands mining. It provided incentives for oil companies to drill in the Gulf of Mexico and other subsidies for the oil and nuclear industries. One of the most controversial aspects of the Energy Policy Act of 2005 was to exempt oil and gas producers from certain requirements of the Clean Water Act, the Clean Air Act, and the Safe Drinking Water Act.

Known as the Halliburton loophole, the provision stripped the Environmental Protection Agency (EPA) of its authority to regulate hydraulic fracturing, commonly known as fracking, which is a drilling process that involves injecting water, sand, and chemicals into underground rock formations to release natural gas deposits. Invented in 1940 by the Halliburton corporation, fracking has been very effective in areas where the geological formations have made it difficult for conventional drilling operations.

It also has been a very controversial practice. Fracking has been implicated in a growing number of pollution cases across the country. The fluid used in the fracking process contains highly toxic chemicals that, in some cases, have come to contaminate water and leach into nearby land. Toxic fumes have been released into the air, affecting humans, pets, and wildlife. The Halliburton loophole exempts companies from disclosing the mixture of chemicals used in fracking operations—chemicals that could be the source of serious environmental pollution and public health problems.

The fracking industry defends the Halliburton loophole by underscoring the effectiveness and safety of the fracking process. The combination of chemicals used by different energy companies, the industry argues, should remain proprietary secrets because revealing them would hurt competitiveness. Furthermore, energy industry officials contend that any additional layers of regulation would stifle innovation and inhibit domestic drilling, which would hurt America's energy independence.

Critics of the Halliburton loophole counter that if the process is so safe, companies shouldn't hesitate to disclose the information. They argue that the public has a right to know the mix of toxic chemicals being used in the fracking process, many of which have found their way into the nation's water supply, contaminating water and adversely affecting public health.

In 2009 the Fracturing Responsibility and Awareness of Chemicals Act, also known as the FRAC Act, was first introduced to both houses of the US Congress. The bill would close the Halliburton loophole by requiring companies to disclose the chemical formulas used in hydraulic fracking operations. It would also restore the EPA's authority to regulate the industry.

The 2009 bill stalled in Congress and was reintroduced in 2011. However, the FRAC Act stalled in Congress once again and was reintroduced in 2013, where it encountered significant opposition from the drilling industry. The safety of fracking is one of the topics discussed in the following chapter, which examines how chemicals endanger the nation's water and food supply. Other viewpoints in the chapter explore the risk from chemical spills and pesticides, as well as the value of chemical dispersants used in large oil spills.

"*While the recent events in West Virginia—a chemical tank leaking into a
river just upstream of a regional water
plant's intake source—seem like a rare
confluence of factors threatening water
quality, it would be foolhardy to ignore
this as a one-off event.*"

How Safe Is
Our Drinking Water?

James Salzman

James Salzman is the author of Drinking Water: A History *and
a professor of law and environmental history at Duke University.
In the following viewpoint, he evaluates the danger from three
broad classes of threats to the nation's water supply: natural contaminants, which do not pose a serious threat because authorities have become adept at handling biological pathogens; intentional attacks on the water supply, which remain a threat but
are closely monitored; and chemical spills, which are the most
dangerous threat to the nation's water. Salzman discusses a 2014
chemical spill in Charleston, West Virginia, that dumped an industrial chemical used for treating coal into the city's water sup-*

ply. Authorities were forced to cut off water to hundreds of thousands of people. Salzman argues that improved monitoring is vital in such situations and that authorities must identify the contaminants quickly and take the proper precautions to protect public health and the environment.

As you read, consider the following questions:

1. According to Salzman, how many residents were impacted by the January 2014 chemical spill into the Elk River?

2. How much water do reservoirs hold, according to the author?

3. How many times a year does New York City test its tap water for contaminants, according to the author?

The area around Charleston, W.Va., has been brought to its knees by contaminated drinking water. Thousands of gallons of an industrial chemical used for treating coal, MCHM [4-methylcyclohexane methanol], leaked last week [January 9, 2014] from a company's steel tank, flowed down the bank and into the Elk River, located just a mile upriver from the intake point for the region's drinking water treatment plant.

Residents quickly noticed the licorice smell and a few hours later were officially warned not to drink or cook, wash, or bathe with the water. A state of emergency was declared in nine counties. Schools, hospitals, restaurants, hotels, and more closed. About 300,000 residents were affected.

A Vital Question

We take the quality of our drinking water for granted, and for good reason. More people in the United States have access to safe water than ever before. Yet recent events raise an obvious concern: How safe is our drinking water really?

This question is both timely and timeless, for water providers have constantly defended water sources against contamination. From well before the Romans through today, they have always faced three broad classes of threats.

The first comes from natural contaminants—pathogens we expect to find in water. Despite images of clear, burbling springs and mountain streams, the simple fact is that fresh water is just not very clean. Teeming parasites, viruses, and bacteria live in water. Just a hundred years ago, dying from waterborne typhoid or cholera was commonplace in the United States, and deadly epidemics still break out in some parts of the world today. The addition of chlorine to water supplies a century ago largely eliminated these scourges. We have since become very good at eliminating biological pathogens with chlorination, ozonation, ultraviolet radiation, and filtration as redundant lines of defense. Nonetheless, vigilance remains necessary. Just two decades ago, a treatment plant piped contaminated water to Milwaukee residents, sickening one-quarter of the city's population. Sixty-nine people died.

Intentional attack presents the second class of threat. While Sept. 11 [referring to the terrorist attacks against the United States on September 11, 2001] focused immediate attention on drinking water, these are hardly new concerns. Poisoning the enemy is a long-standing military strategy. When Solon of Athens laid siege to Cirrha circa 600 B.C., he ordered that poisonous hellebore roots be placed in the local water supply, making the Cirrhaeans violently sick. In 1941, concerned over domestic attacks from Nazi or Japanese agents, J. Edgar Hoover warned about the vulnerability of water supply facilities "due to the strategic position they occupy in keeping the wheels of industry turning and in preserving the health and morale of the American populace."

There have not been any successful major attacks on American water supplies, but the threat and fear remain because our water supplies cannot be fully protected. We could erect more fences, higher fences, locks, security cameras, and hire more guards—and we have—but with more than 75,000 dams and reservoirs, more than 160,000 drinking water facilities, mostly owned and operated by local government and private parties, 2 million miles of pipe and millions more access points, these measures will never make us completely safe. Our water systems present an impossibly big target to protect from intentional acts or accidents.

The good news is that poisoning a water system is hard to do. Putting a few drops of cyanide in someone's glass will lead to a gruesome death. Putting a few drops, or even a few barrels, in a reservoir is pointless. Reservoirs generally hold anywhere from 3 million to 30 million gallons of water. Even assuming one could back several trucks up to the reservoir and dump their loads without being detected, one would still need to get huge quantities of the poison in the first place. The Department of Homeland Security keeps track of biological and chemical agents that might be used by terrorists, and these substances are not easy to come by in large quantities.

The Danger of Chemical Spills

The last class of threat comes from accidents, as occurred in West Virginia. In many respects these are the most difficult to plan for because there are so many potential contaminants. The MCHM passed directly through the treatment plant into water mains because the plant was not designed to deal with this chemical. It's not supposed to be in our water. Nor are the thousands of other hazardous chemicals stored and transported around the country. Many tanks are located near a river or lake intentionally, to make transport cheaper. But accidents happen—tanks can leak, trains can derail. Hence the challenge for water suppliers is how to protect against low-probability/high-impact events.

Monitoring Threats to the Water Supply

Because our overall water system from headwaters to tap is simply too large to prevent any contamination, either inten-

"Have we been dumping chemicals in the swamp?"

© Andrew Toos/CartoonStock.com.

tional or accidental, it becomes critical to detect threats quickly, identify the contaminants, and take proper precautions so people don't drink the water. As a result, improved monitoring is where much of the current action lies.

The town of Loveland, Colo., for example, keeps a tank of drinking water full of trout. When the trout start to die, the water managers know something is wrong with the water and investigate. Bigger systems take multiple measurements at different points in the system every day. Following the Sept. 11 attacks, New York City increased the number of daily water samples. It now tests its tap water more than 330,000 times each year.

The next generation of sensitive monitors will detect a range of contaminants in real time. DNA microchip arrays, immunological techniques, micro-robots, flow cytometry, and molecular probes and other emerging technologies could be placed throughout the water system to provide rapid warning of contaminants early enough to allow quick responses by water authorities.

A utility could harden infrastructure. It may extend distribution pipes or build two treatment plants instead of one, allowing it to draw water from different sources during an emergency. Pipes may be buried instead of elevated. Virtually every construction choice, in fact, might look different if security became a top design priority.

Former New York City mayor Michael Bloomberg has stated the challenge clearly: "Our drinking water really is the lifeblood of this city, and that, unfortunately, might make it a target for sabotage. We need to be vigilant in protecting our water systems." This is equally true for accidents. Left unsaid, though, is a vexing challenge.

Underfunded Systems

As with so many policy issues, knowing what to do is only half the battle. You also have to pay for it. System hardening and improved monitoring are expensive. Emerging detection technologies are unlikely to be developed commercially if the market payoff appears small.

Our water systems, though, remain deeply underfunded. A water main bursts somewhere in the country every two minutes. Some cities have pipes that were laid just after the Civil War. In this budget-conscious environment, upgrading plants to treat for every imaginable chemical is not going to happen, nor perhaps should it.

While it's an obvious question, asking whether our drinking water is vulnerable is not really helpful. It is vulnerable. The question is how vulnerable, and how great the risk of harm compared with other potential threats.

Our water systems are well-designed to prevent natural contaminants from getting into the pipes and coming out of the tap. Poisoning from large-scale attacks remains difficult, given the precautions already in place and the sheer volumes needed to poison a large water supply. Accidents, though, give special cause for concern.

A Pressing Concern

While the recent events in West Virginia—a chemical tank leaking into a river just upstream of a regional water plant's intake source—may seem like a rare confluence of factors threatening water quality, it would be foolhardy to ignore this as a one-off event. At least two lessons should be clear.

First, we need to pay closer attention to the structural integrity of chemical storage near water bodies. At a time of reduced agency budgets and pressure for deregulation, we need to acknowledge that officials ensuring compliance with health and safety regulations, such as tank safety requirements, keep us safe. Second, water authorities need the resources to ensure effective detection and rapid communication. These are critical in minimizing harm when threats do arise.

Benjamin Franklin wrote that "when the well's dry, we know the worth of water." He also observed that "an ounce of prevention is worth a pound of cure." We would do well to remember both.

| *"As regulators grapple with the lethal dangers of pesticides, scientists are discovering that even seemingly benign, low-level exposures to pesticides can affect wild creatures in subtle, unexpected ways—and could even be contributing to a rash of new epidemics pushing species to the brink of extinction."*

The Use of Chemical Pesticides Endangers Wildlife and the Environment

Sonia Shah

Sonia Shah is an author and a science reporter. In the following viewpoint, she reports that three recent epidemics that have devastated populations of amphibians, bees, and bats can be traced to low-level exposure to pesticides. Toxicologists believe that these seemingly benign levels of pesticide impair immune function in wildlife, leading to outbreaks of disease. In these recent die-offs, millions of amphibians, bees, and bats have died over several years, decimating local populations. Shah suggests that the correlation between low levels of pesticides and die-offs is notoriously difficult to prove conclusively; in some areas, more than one pesticide has been used, and habitats are complex and subject to various factors. These epidemics, she argues, are providing a wealth of new information on how pesticides affect the environment.

As you read, consider the following questions:

1. According to the author, what percentage of major US rivers and streams are contaminated with pesticides?

2. What percentage of the US honeybee population does the author report was devastated by colony collapse disorder?

3. How many bats have been killed by the white-nose syndrome from 2006 to 2010, according to Shah?

Ever since Olga Owen Huckins shared the spectacle of a yard full of dead, DDT [dichlorodiphenyltrichloroethane]-poisoned birds with her friend Rachel Carson in 1958, scientists have been tracking the dramatic toll on wildlife of a planet awash in pesticides. Today, drips and puffs of pesticides surround us everywhere, contaminating 90 percent of the nation's major rivers and streams, more than 80 percent of sampled fish, and one-third of the nation's aquifers. According to the U.S. Fish and Wildlife Service, fish and birds that unsuspectingly expose themselves to this chemical soup die by the millions every year.

New Epidemics

But as regulators grapple with the lethal dangers of pesticides, scientists are discovering that even seemingly benign, low-level exposures to pesticides can affect wild creatures in subtle, unexpected ways—and could even be contributing to a rash of new epidemics pushing species to the brink of extinction.

In the past dozen years, no fewer than three never-before-seen diseases have decimated populations of amphibians, bees, and—most recently—bats. A growing body of evidence indicates that pesticide exposure may be playing an important role in the decline of the first two species, and scientists are investigating whether such exposures may be involved in the deaths of more than 1 million bats in the northeastern United States over the past several years.

For decades, toxicologists have accrued a range of evidence showing that low-level pesticide exposure impairs immune function in wildlife, and have correlated this immune damage to outbreaks of disease. Consumption of pesticide-contaminated herring has been found to impair the immune function of captive seals, for example, and may have contributed to an outbreak of distemper that killed over 18,000 harbor seals along the northern European coast in 1988. Exposure to PCBs [polychlorinated biphenyls] has been correlated with higher levels of roundworm infection in Arctic seagulls. The popular herbicide atrazine has been shown to make tadpoles more susceptible to parasitic worms.

The Effect of the Chytrid Fungus

The recent spate of widespread die-offs began in amphibians. Scientists discovered the culprit—an aquatic fungus called *Batrachochytrium dendrobatidis*, of a class of fungi called "chytrids"—in 1998. Its devastation, says amphibian expert Kevin Zippel, is "unlike anything we've seen since the extinction of the dinosaurs." Over 1,800 species of amphibians currently face extinction.

It may be, as many experts believe, that the chytrid fungus is a novel pathogen, decimating species that have no armor against it, much as Europe's smallpox and measles decimated Native Americans in the sixteenth and seventeenth centuries. But "there is a really good plausible story of chemicals affecting the immune system and making animals more susceptible," as well, says San Francisco State University conservation biologist Carlos Davidson.

A Troubling Correlation

In California, for example, insecticides coated on the crops of the San Joaquin Valley are known to waft upwind to the Sierra Nevada mountains, where they settle in the air, snow, and surface waters, and inside the tissues of amphibians. And when Davidson compared historical reports of pesticide use, habitat loss, wind patterns, and amphibian population counts in California for the years 1971 to 1991, he found a strong correlation between upwind pesticide use—in particular cholinesterase-inhibiting chemicals such as the insecticide carbaryl—and declining amphibian populations.

Experimental evidence bolsters Davidson's findings. In lab experiments, exposure to carbaryl dramatically reduced yellow-legged frogs' production of fungus-fighting compounds called antimicrobial peptides, which may be crucial to amphibians' ability to fend off chytrid fungus. Further testing has shown that amphibian species that produce the most effective mixes of antimicrobial peptides resist experimental chytrid infection, and tend to be those that survive most successfully in the wild.

Colony Collapse Disorder

Six years after scientists discovered the fungal assault on amphibians, a mysterious plague began decimating honeybees. Foraging honeybees first started vanishing from their hives, abandoning their broods and queens to certain death by starvation, in 2004. Alarmed beekeepers dubbed the devastating malady "colony collapse disorder." Between 2006 and 2009, colony collapse disorder and other ills destroyed 35 percent of the U.S. honeybee population.

Some experts believe colony collapse disorder is the result of a "perfect storm" of honeybee-debilitating factors: poor nutrition, immune dysfunction from decades of industrial beekeeping practices, and the opportunism of multiple pathogens, acting in malevolent concert. But many beekeepers

What Are Pesticides?

Pesticides are a broad class of chemicals and biological agents that are specifically designed and applied to kill a pest. Specific types of pesticides target specific types of pests: insecticides kill insects, fungicides kill fungi and bacteria, herbicides kill weeds and other unwanted plant vegetation, molluscicides kill mollusks, acaricides kill spiders, and so on. Pesticide use dates back to ancient times.

Pesticides are regulated in the United States at both the federal and state level. The primary legislation, one of the oldest environmental laws, is the Federal Insecticide, Fungicide, and Rodenticide Act (FIFRA, 1972), which is administered by the Environmental Protection Agency (EPA). Each state also has an agency responsible for carrying out FIFRA mandates. These agencies may be environmental or agricultural in nature, depending on the state. State laws can be more restrictive than the federal laws.

Pesticides are sometimes called "economic poisons." They are developed to kill something, and they are, therefore, inherently toxic. Pesticides that are less toxic are classified as "general use pesticides." These can be purchased by the average homeowner and applied without any special license or permits. More toxic compounds are called "restricted use pesticides" and their use requires a license. In some cases the restricted use materials have the same active ingredients as the general use materials, but at a higher concentration.

Anything that claims that it has pesticidal activity is, by law, a pesticide, and is subject to registration by the EPA and local state agencies.

Mark G. Robson, "Pesticides,"
Encyclopedia of Public Health, *2002.*

believe that a new class of chemicals based on nicotine, called neonicotinoids, may be to blame.

Neonicotinoids

Neonicotinoids came into wide use in the early 2000s. Unlike older pesticides that evaporate or disperse shortly after application, neonicotinoids are systemic poisons. Applied to the soil or doused on seeds, neonicotinoid insecticides incorporate themselves into the plant's tissues, turning the plant itself into a tiny poison factory emitting toxin from its roots, leaves, stems, pollen, and nectar.

In Germany, France, Italy, and Slovenia, beekeepers' concerns about neonicotinoids' effect on bee colonies have resulted in a series of bans on the chemicals. In the United States, regulators have approved their use, despite the fact that the Environmental Protection Agency's standard method of protecting bees from insecticides—by requiring farmers to refrain from applying them during blooming times when bees are most exposed—does little to protect bees from systemic pesticides.

"The companies believe this stuff is safe," says U.S. Department of Agriculture (USDA) entomologist Jeff Pettis. "It is used at lower levels, and is a boon for farmers," since neonicotinoids don't require repeated application, nor wide broadcasting into the environment, he explains. Plus, years of research have shown that only very low levels of the chemicals are exuded from the pollen and nectar of treated plants.

But University of Padua entomologist Vincenzo Girolami believes he may have discovered an unexpected mechanism by which neonicotinoids—despite their novel mode of application—do in fact kill bees. In the spring, neonicotinoid-coated seeds are planted using seeding machines, which kick up clouds of insecticide into the air. "The cloud is 20 meters wide, sometimes 50 meters, and the machines go up and down and up and down," he says. "Bees that cross the fields, making a trip every ten minutes, have a high probability of encountering this cloud. If they make a trip every five minutes, it is certain that they will encounter this cloud."

And the result could be immediately devastating. In as-yet-unpublished research, Girolami has found concentrations of insecticide in clouds above seeding machines 1,000 times the dose lethal to bees. In the spring, when the seed machines are working, says Girolami, "I think that 90 percent or more of deaths of bees is due to direct pesticide poisoning."

Girolami has also found lethal levels of neonicotinoids in other, unexpected—and usually untested—places, such as the drops of liquid that treated crops secrete along their leaf margins, which bees and other insects drink. (The scientific community has yet to weigh in on Girolami's new, still-to-be-published research, but Pettis, who has heard of the work, calls it "a good and plausible explanation.")

The White-Nose Syndrome

Two years after the honeybees started disappearing, so, too, did bats. The corpses of hibernating bats were first found blanketing caves in the northeastern United States in 2006. The disease that killed them, caused by a cold-loving fungus called *Geomyces destructans* [presently known as *Pseudogymnoascus destructans*]—and dubbed white-nose syndrome for the tell-tale white fuzz it leaves on bats' ears and noses—has since destroyed at least one million bats. University of Florida wildlife ecologist John Hayes calls it "the most precipitous wildlife decline in the past century in North America."

Like the mysterious *Batrachochytrium dendrobatidis* fungus infesting amphibians, *Geomyces* could be a novel pathogen, newly preying upon defenseless bat species. But scientists have also started to investigate whether pesticide exposure might be playing a role.

Bats are especially vulnerable to chemical pollution. They're small—the little brown bat weighs just 8 grams—and can live for up to three decades. "That's lots of time to accumulate pesticides and contaminants," points out Boston University bat researcher and PhD candidate Marianne Moore, who is studying whether environmental contaminants suppress bats' immune function. "We know they are exposed to and accumulate organochlorines, mercury, arsenic, lead, dioxins," she says, "but we don't understand the effects."

Which, in the end, is the central dilemma facing pesticide-reliant societies. Proving, with statistical certainty, that low-level pesticide exposure makes living things more vulnerable to disease is notoriously difficult. There are too many different pesticides, lurking in too many complex, poorly understood habitats to build definitively damning indictments. The evidence is subtle, suggestive. But with the rapid decimation of amphibians, bees, and bats, it is accumulating, fast.

"*Both the American public and our corporate and political leaders need to face the facts. It's just not possible for everyone to have their cake and eat it, too.*"

Chemicals Involved in Fracking Are a Public Health Risk

Sandy Dechert

Sandy Dechert is a blogger and writer. In the following viewpoint, she explores an Associated Press (AP) report that four states—Ohio, Pennsylvania, West Virginia, and Texas—found evidence that hydraulic fracturing, commonly referred to as fracking, has caused considerable water pollution near oil and gas wells. The AP investigation found that there were thousands of complaints of pollution in these four states, with several confirmed by state investigators. The pollution caused by fracking is associated with a range of severe health problems, including cancer, respiratory problems, neurological issues, and a higher rate of birth defects. Now that it has been established that fracking has contaminated community water supplies, Dechert deems it vital that state governments establish better and more standardized reporting of fracking pollution and greater transparency with the public.

As you read, consider the following questions:

1. According to a 2012 survey from the University of Texas, what percentage of Americans have no idea how fracking works?

2. How many wells are fracked each year, according to the Environmental Protection Agency (EPA)?

3. According to Dechert, what is the amount of recoverable gas estimated for Pennsylvania alone?

Four states—Pennsylvania, Ohio, West Virginia, and Texas—have confirmed that hydraulic fracturing, also called "fracking," has caused water pollution near oil and gas wells.

The Associated Press released these state government findings on Sunday [in January 2014]. . . .

But how well did the public understand what was important in the AP report? Probably not very well. A survey from the University of Texas [UT] about twice the size of Gallup's usual weekly polls, conducted in mid-2012 but quoted as recently as 15 months later, and with age, sex, race/ethnicity, education, region, and household income weighted where necessary to reflect the actual U.S. population, revealed that almost two-thirds of Americans have no idea how fracking works.

What Is Fracking?

Widely used in North America over the past decade, fracking is a petroleum mining method that injects a huge, highly pressurized mixture of water, sand, and chemicals deep into the earth to break up dense shale rock and release oil and/or gas formerly trapped in it. The mining practice involves nonrenewable and polluting fuels. Thus it does not fit current definitions of "clean" and "green," although when used for power, fracked gas pollutes less than coal or gasoline.

Environmental groups and some politicians believe that fracking could cause environmental damage, including effects on climate and human health. They foresee impacts caused by the rough physics involved (which has been linked to earthquakes in previously non-seismic areas) and due to the use of biocides to kill belowground bacteria, lubricants for smooth product pumping and scale inhibitors to reduce minerals that inevitably clog transport pipes.

Some deride fracking for reducing natural or built areas into seemingly meaningless webs of dirt roads, creating fast wealth, and reinventing previously civilized settlements—all to be deserted when the resources are exhausted and boom turns to bust. Most of the vaunted "new" jobs created by fracking last only through the exploration and construction phases of development.

Industry, other politicians, and often government hail the recently adopted mining practice as re-enabling America's national status and contributing toward our energy independence. The 2010 IHS Cambridge Energy Research Associates report "Fueling North America's Energy Future" has estimated that natural gas, which provides almost 25% of the U.S. energy supply, could meet half of our needs by 2035. Since President [Barack] Obama is still holding firm to an "all of the above" energy mix, fracking is not likely to go away any time soon.

Scope of the AP's Investigation

For their study, AP researchers requested data from Pennsylvania, Ohio, West Virginia, and Texas, all states heavily involved in the recent surge of oil and gas drilling, about complaints related to hydraulic fracking for oil and gas.

Although multinational oil companies drill thousands of wells across the U.S. without incident each year, AP discovered that hundreds of drilling-related objections have been filed in these four states. The complaints also revealed major differences in state reporting.

Lindsay Abrams revealed the crux of the problem in her article in *Salon* Tuesday [January 6, 2014]:

> For a process that's driving America's energy boom, the things we don't know about fracking for oil and natural gas often seem to surpass that which we do. . . . Leaving aside the fact that gas and oil companies aren't required to disclose exactly which [of the hundreds of] chemicals they're using, actual information about water contamination's scope and severity . . . is hard to come by.

The main concern here is not the existence of pollution reports. Almost 2,500 have been cited by officials in four different states. Pollution has been publicly confirmed in some of these cases, and in a handful, the oil and gas companies responsible for doing the fracking have attempted to clean up their errors.

The issue is that the scattershot nature of formal reporting may be confusing or misleading the press and the public. Here are some of the statistics that the states have confirmed from their fracking reports:

—Pennsylvania: at least 106 water-well contamination cases since 2005, out of more than 5,000 new wells. Almost half of these infractions occurred between 2012 and third quarter 2012. The commonwealth has no private water-well construction standards. [Pennsylvania] Department of Environmental Protection [DEP] spokeswoman Lisa Kasianowitz said two of the reports showed fracking linked to human health problems. Three of the investigations continue. According to AP, "the department has argued in court filings that it does not count how many contamination 'determination letters' it issues or track where they are kept in its files."

—Ohio: six confirmed cases of contamination since 2010 out of 204 reports. Fourteen of these are still under investigation. Ohio Department of Natural Resources spokesman Mark Bruce reportedly said that none of these was related to fracking.

—West Virginia: 122 complaints of drilling-caused water-well contamination since 2010. Four of these were so compelling that the driller(s) agreed to take corrective action, officials said.

—Texas, the most widely mined state: more than 2,000 complaints. Of these, 62 directly allege possible well-water contamination from oil and gas activity. Texas officials produced a detailed 94-page spreadsheet that included the date of each complaint, the landowner, the drilling company, and a summary of the alleged problems. Ramona Nye, a spokeswoman for the state drilling authority (Railroad Commission of Texas), provided this information but was unable to confirm any proven cases of drilling-related water-well contamination in the past 10 years.

The problem worsens because when leasing underground rights to drill, oil and gas companies often require nondisclosure from the surface owners. This practice prohibits those who actually own the property (and lease out their subsurface rights) from discussing problems that come up during the fracking process. And as AP points out, the different requirements of states for reporting fracking issues only muddy an already obscure national picture.

"Right or wrong," scientist Rob Jackson of Duke University told the AP, "many people in the public feel like [Pennsylvania] DEP is stonewalling some of these investigations." Accurate information is difficult or impossible to obtain. Similar problems plague the other three states, and almost certainly affect fracking states not under investigation as well.

How Fracking Affects the Environment

As noted earlier, over 60 percent of respondents to the 2012 UT survey did not know how fracking works. The process uses huge amounts of fresh water to flush out deep oil and gas reserves: between 2 and 4 million gallons each time a well is fracked. The water may come from nearby supplies, if they are adequate, or the drillers may have it trucked in. EPA estimates that about 35,000 wells are fracked each year. The amount used in annual drilling could thus supply five million people per year with drinking water.

Some "produced water" (flow-back waste, or industry-injected chemicals, which comprise half to two percent of the fracking fluids, that mix with the salty, slightly radioactive water that occurs naturally within the shale layers) pumps out along with the desired petroleum. All these pollutants can and sometimes do seep into adjacent sources of drinking water. Environmentalists, landowners, conscientious public servants, and others worry that local drinking water supplies could be contaminated.

Hydraulic extraction has been a known drilling technology not for 10 years, but for many decades. However, the practice of fracking did not become profitable for petroleum companies until energy prices recently skyrocketed. Then the technological advances needed to drill deep and directionally underground became affordable to industry.

A widely cited September 2013 report called "America's New Energy Future: The Unconventional Oil and Gas Revolution and the US Economy" has an industry-friendly view of the history and potential. According to IHS, the global information company that produced the study, the recent U.S. increase in unconventional oil and natural gas extraction added an average of $1,200 in discretionary income to each American household in 2012. Petroleum drilling for energy now reportedly supports 1.2 million jobs, a total projected to increase to 3.3 million by the end of this decade.

Denise Robbins of Media Matters for America notes that these figures and estimates greatly exceed the findings of previous studies. Robbins also points out that quite a few major news outlets, including Reuters, CNBC, *Forbes*, and the *Los Angeles Times*, covered the IHS report without mentioning the company's financial ties to petroleum and related industries. America's Natural Gas Alliance, the American Petroleum Institute, the American Chemistry Council, the Natural Gas Supply Association, and similar groups all had a part in funding the bullish study.

Does Fracking Cause Human Health Problems?

The political element and the popular press exploit this question. The recent trend toward "false balance" in news reporting from television and press has created the impression that the subject involves considerable debate.

The Checks and Balances Project has implicated these factors in the growth of false balance thinking:

- Growing influence of the corporate lobbying industry.

- Declining size of the press corps available to fact-check and accurately describe that industry.

- Severe time impoverishment in newsrooms caused by drastic cutbacks in the size and depth of the press corps, combined with the acute new time pressures of blogging, iterative reporting, and tweeting.

- Ultra-technical nature of energy and environmental issues, which enables charlatans to cloud the debate and crowd out honest brokers, such as the National Renewable Energy Laboratory, with authoritative-sounding pronouncements.

The Politics of Fracking

Politicians have oversimplified the issue of pollution and human health in the fracking debate and have sharpened their arguments accordingly. Each side now tends toward simply demonizing the other. Here are several relatively plain examples of loose health statements on the anti-fracking side:

Along with this fracking-enabled oil and gas rush have come troubling reports of poisoned drinking water, polluted air, mysterious animal deaths, industrial disasters and explosions. We call them "Fraccidents."

Health consequences of concern include infertility, birth defects, and cancer.

And a more grounded conclusion from the AP study:

People who live close to natural gas drilling in four states complain of similar health symptoms, ranging from respiratory infections to lesions and neurological [disorders]. . . .

Compare to these the pro-fracking bias involved in a popular University of Texas at Austin examination of fracking made in concert with the inappropriately named Environmental Defense Fund [EDF]. EDF's "oddly rosy findings" won praise from the American Petroleum Institute, Energy in Depth, the propaganda film *FrackNation*, and The Blaze, a conservative news website founded by Glenn Beck.

"It seems plausible the industry-stacked committee drove the report in a direction beneficial to oil industry profits rather than science," critics of the EDF report have responded.

Different Approaches to Fracking

In most of the states involved with fracking, legislation and public sentiment have swung back and forth on the issues. Some, like Texas and Pennsylvania, now look to shale gas as a deficit-busting revenue source. More than $500 billion in recoverable gas have been estimated for Pennsylvania alone.

Other states are taking a more cautious approach. Some have tried moratoria and regulatory measures such as not issuing drilling permits without allowing time for an adequate assessment of the situation. After all, regulators note, those petroleum reserves aren't going to fade away in the time it takes to look at things a little more carefully. But political dif-

Fracking

Developed in 1947, induced hydraulic fracturing, also referred to as hydrofracking or fracking, has become a prevalent and controversial means of extracting petroleum and natural gas trapped in rocks beneath the earth's surface. For fifty years fracking was used primarily to release natural gas trapped in sandstone deposits. In the late 1990s, however, scientists with Mitchell Energy and Development created a commercially viable method of fracking for extracting natural gas and petroleum from shale, a highly porous but lowly permeable rock containing hydrocarbons. Since the development of this process, known as horizontal slickwater hydraulic fracturing, the use of fracking has grown exponentially, and energy companies have drilled hundreds of thousands of new wells. Environmental groups and many people living near these operations, however, oppose fracking because of potential environmental and human health concerns. In March 2014, a group of six organizations in the United Kingdom published a report titled "Are We Fit to Frack?," which detailed the potential environmental impact of fracking and called for a ban on fracking in ecologically sensitive areas.

"Fracking,"
Global Issues in Context Online Collection, 2014.

ferences among governors, state legislatures, and local officials and stage-managed public outrage tend to heat up the controversy.

> "We need to appreciate what we're getting ourselves into," says Robert K. Sweeney, chairman of the New York State Assembly Standing Committee on Envi-

ronmental Conservation. "It's not just the pumping of chemicals into the ground or the air pollution, it's also the effect on quality of life—something as simple as truck traffic, which other states didn't consider when they issued permits. I'd like to see a cost-benefit analysis that considers the upside of fracking—the jobs, the revenues—but also the downside in terms of loss of property values and health impacts. There's a lot to this issue that argues for taking our time. The gas isn't going anywhere, so what's the rush? If we do it, we should do it right."

In the end, Drs. Madelon L. Finkel and Adam Law of Weill Cornell Medical College may have summarized what we may need to know about the bottom line on fracking versus demonstrable health risks. Their May 2011 article for the *American Journal of Public Health*, "The Rush to Drill for Natural Gas: A Public Health Cautionary Tale," provides a broad overview of the medical effects of aggressive drilling for oil and gas:

> Little research has been done on the potential adverse health effects of fracking. Roxana Witter et al. reviewed the available literature, which showed evidence of risk to human health ranging from the comparatively benign to the more serious. One study, based on Pennsylvania Department of Environmental Protection and the Susquehanna River Basin Commission material safety data sheets for 41 products used in fracturing operations, assessed the chemicals used in fracturing and found that 73% of the products had between 6 and 14 different adverse health effects, including skin, eye, and sensory organ damage; respiratory distress, including asthma; gastrointestinal and liver disease; brain and nervous system harms; cancers; and negative reproductive effects.

Some of the negative health effects appeared fairly soon after exposure, whereas others appeared months or years later. . . . Of concern is that endocrine-disrupting chemicals may alter developmental pathways, manifesting decades after exposure or even trans-generationally by altering epigenetic pathways. Hydrofracking fluid and flow-back fluids contain candidate endocrine disruptors, but because of the lack of disclosure by the drilling companies of the individual chemicals with their unique Chemical Abstracts Service registry numbers . . . it is difficult to truly assess their potential adverse effects, and so the cumulative exposure impact is not known.

Vincent M.B. Silenzio, MD, MPH, FRSM, FNYAM, who is a practitioner, public health expert, and triple-tenured professor at the University of Rochester Medical Center School of Medicine and Dentistry, had a striking and unusual comment about the fracking/public health debate. Interviewed yesterday, he said:

"From a public health perspective, I think we need to account for both the direct costs to human health and the indirect costs, such as those incurred through environmental damage that influence human health down the line. Right now, a precise accounting of these costs is beyond what current science can pinpoint. But in my view, any policy discussion about fracking must absolutely include a frank admission that someone in the future will be footing the bill for these costs. If we ultimately decide that the benefits of hydraulic fracturing outweigh the risks and the costs, we will need to decide how to pay for those costs."

What Can We Do to Resolve the Conundrums?

Proof that hydraulic fracturing for oil and "clean gas" can contaminate community water supplies is now public, thanks to Sunday's AP report. It behooves all of us to commit ourselves to the truth, no matter how hard it hurts or personal priorities. Everyone with a stake in the issue needs to "man up."

We clearly need better and more standardized reporting of unusual incidents, from the industry first and confirmed by government. Much greater transparency would be laudable, with real penalties for insufficient documentation. We may not have to take this as far as China, where public officials can be fined or jailed for incomplete or deliberately false disclosure, but we do have to pay closer attention.

Health effects should be highlighted in project reporting: location and duration of incidents, nature of health problems, how many people are potentially affected, and so on.

We need better energy education. The public can't make policy decisions about controversies in the absence of information (including even the very existence of debated practices). Marketing strategy and advertising too easily promote false assumptions about the scope of the drilling process.

Both the American public and our corporate and political leaders need to face the facts. It's just not possible for everyone to have their cake and eat it, too.

Especially in Europe, countries have voted to outlaw hydraulic fracturing. Less dramatic measures we could adopt include regulations with teeth, amending local and state laws, curtailing transport of hazardous fossil fuels, limiting the time in which companies with exploration permits can progress without serious environmental planning, disallowing lawsuits by oil companies on specious procedural complaints, implementing carbon trading that works, and a dreaded but fair and probably inevitable tax on producers of fossil fuels.

If we are committed to renewable energy like wind and solar to eliminate the demonstrated short- and long-term health effects of drilling (not to mention the ultimately fatal climate effects), we must advocate for these higher principles from the grassroots to the boardroom to the international bargaining table.

We must shut up those on any side who demonize their opponents while ignoring the scientific debate. We must silence the mindless protestations that scientific researchers are just seeking grant money on hot topics. Accusations like these are simply irrelevant and inflammatory in the absence of proof.

Finally, we should consider incentivizing straight talk instead of subsidizing untruths.

"The year just passed will definitely be remembered as a time when oil and natural gas markets started changing quickly and perceptions about America's role in world energy markets changed as well," a publicly funded newscaster declared during the last days of 2013.

Many other important issues surround fracking that do not involve the health trade-off. Among them: water scarcity, ethics of ownership and profit, international security, and climate change. We cannot be certain how to weigh health among them, but we have to start somewhere. The hidden costs of the past decade's boom in fossil drilling are starting to emerge.

"All chemicals used in the fracking process have common applications from swimming pool cleaners and laundry detergents to cosmetics, and even ice cream."

Fracking Is Not a Public Health Risk

Nicolas D. Loris

Nicolas D. Loris is an economist and a fellow at the Heritage Foundation. In the following viewpoint, he elucidates the positive economic aspects of hydraulic fracturing, also known as fracking, in the United States and challenges some of the misconceptions surrounding the industry. Loris underscores the importance of fracking to the nation's energy future, regarding it as vital for job creation and energy independence. He argues that although there has been much concern over polluted drinking water because of the chemical additives used in fracking, the process is safe and public health is not at risk. In fact, he explains, many of the chemical additives used in the fracking process are regulated by the state and have common household applications. Loris maintains that it would be unnecessary and counterproductive for the federal government to further regulate fracking, and Congress should take steps to ensure that the industry continues to grow.

Nicolas D. Loris, "Hydraulic Fracturing: Critical for Energy Production, Jobs, and Economic Growth," The Heritage Foundation, August 28, 2012.

As you read, consider the following questions:

1. According to Loris, how many US states allow oil and gas production?

2. What percentage of US electricity does Loris cite as provided by natural gas?

3. How many instances of seismic activity had been reported as of 2012 because of fracking activity, according to the author?

While Americans continue to be disappointed by dismal jobs reports and a high unemployment rate, one of the few recent bright spots in the U.S. economy has been energy production, particularly the shale oil and shale gas revolution. In fact, the Yale Graduates Energy Study Group calculated that in 2010 alone, the consumer surplus (the consumer savings or gain from reductions in price) from shale gas production was worth over $100 billion. The technological one-two punch of horizontal drilling and hydraulic fracturing has created a remarkable energy boom and created hundreds of thousands of jobs in the U.S. The possibility of continuously low natural gas prices is turning the United States into a prime destination for chemical companies and other businesses that rely on abundant amounts of natural gas. While the energy development has been substantially positive, the process of hydraulic fracturing has come under scrutiny over concerns about contamination of drinking water, the use of chemicals, wastewater management, and the potential for causing earthquakes.

All 35 of the oil- and gas-producing states have an impressive and long track record of regulating hydraulic fracturing, yet the federal government is proposing onerous and duplicative regulations. Congress should recognize the states' effectiveness in regulating hydraulic fracturing and prevent federal attempts that would unreasonably slow down the success of oil and gas development.

How Does Hydraulic Fracturing Work?

Hydraulic fracturing, known as "fracking," is a process during which producers inject a fluid consisting of water, sand, and chemical additives deep into the ground in order to free resources, including oil, natural gas, geothermal energy, and even water trapped in deep rock formations. With respect to shale gas (natural gas lodged in shale rock formations), producers drill wells that are on average 7,500 feet below the surface, thousands of feet below drinking water aquifers. After a company completes the well drilling (approximately two to four weeks), it then fracks the rock formation at high pressures that extend for several hundred feet away from the gas well. This process takes between three and five days, at which point the well will produce natural gas for 20 years to 50 years, or longer. After the drilling, the company also restores the land with soil and new vegetation, leaving only the well head and collection tanks. Some of the fracking fluid rises to the surface through steel-cased well bores and is temporarily stored in lined pits or steel tanks. Companies then recycle and reuse the wastewater or store it in an injection well deep underground.

Used in over one million wells in the United States for more than 60 years, fracking has been successfully used to retrieve more than 7 billion barrels of oil and over 600 trillion cubic feet of natural gas. Just one trillion cubic feet of natural gas is enough to heat 15 million homes for one year. The development of hydraulic fracturing and horizontal drilling has increased access to proven reserves for oil and natural gas in Alabama, Arkansas, Colorado, Illinois, Louisiana, Michigan, New York, North Dakota, Oklahoma, Pennsylvania, Texas, and Wyoming.

Although geologists and energy companies have long been aware of the shale oil and shale gas reserves, the technological advancements in horizontal drilling and hydraulic fracturing are helping some regions of the country extract those resources and buck the economic downturn. In North Dakota, 4,600 wells produced 7.5 million barrels of crude oil in December 2009. In January 2012, North Dakota had 6,600 wells pumping out 16.9 million barrels of oil. In Pennsylvania, natural gas production more than quadrupled between 2009 and 2011. The oil and gas boom has created work for geologists, engineers, rig workers, truck drivers, and pipe welders. That also means a higher demand for restaurants, repair shops, hardware stores, hotels, and laundromats in those areas. Energy production could be a catalyst of economic revitalization across the country, and the fracking process will be essential for the development of America's future oil and gas production.

Fracking: Critical for Economic Growth

Natural gas is already a critical part of America's energy portfolio and consequently a critical part of the country's economic growth. Not only does natural gas provide over 25 percent of electricity generation, natural gas and other gases extracted from natural gas provide a feedstock for fertilizers, chemicals and pharmaceuticals, waste treatment, food processing, fueling industrial boilers, and much more. Although natural gas prices in the United States have historically been volatile, the abundance of shale gas brings the possibility of low, stable prices. North America has approximately 4.2 quadrillion (4,244 trillion) cubic feet of recoverable natural gas that would supply 175 years' worth of natural gas at current consumption rates. Further, the National Petroleum Council estimates that fracking will allow 60 percent to 80 percent of all domestically drilled wells during the next 10 years to remain viable.

The abundance of natural gas makes the United States an attractive place to do business, especially for energy-intensive industries. In what could be a growing trend, Royal Dutch Shell recently announced plans to build a petrochemical plant in western Pennsylvania and cited the proximity to natural gas production as the reason for the location. The $2 billion plant will create 10,000 construction jobs and thousands of permanent jobs for Beaver County, Pennsylvania. A new KPMG analysis of the U.S. chemical industry emphasizes that "[w]ith a new and abundant source of low-cost feedstock, the US market has transformed to become one of the most advantageous markets for chemical production in the world." Shuttered steel towns like Youngstown, Ohio, are seeing a reemergence of manufacturing employment opportunities. In Youngstown, V&M Star, the pipe and tube producer, is building a factory to manufacture seamless pipes for hydraulic fracturing that will employ 350 people.

Hydraulic Fracturing: Facts and Myths

Despite the length of time that hydraulic fracturing has been used, and despite the fact that fracking has helped create a burst in American energy production and economic growth, fracking has received much negative attention due to misreporting and dramatic exaggerations. Much of the public's concern over hydraulic fracturing has been over the possibility of contaminated drinking water, the chemicals used in fracking, the potential to create earthquakes, and wastewater management. Such concerns do not take into account the federal and state laws and regulations that address these very issues. Following are the four most prevalent myths—followed by the facts:

Myth #1: *Hydraulic fracturing threatens underground water sources and has led to the contamination of drinking water.*

Fact: *Hydraulic fracturing is subject to both federal and state regulations, and there have been no instances of fracking causing contamination of drinking water.*

Groundwater aquifers sit thousands of feet above the level at which fracking takes place, and companies construct wells with steel-surface casings and cement barriers to prevent gas migration. Studies by the Environmental Protection Agency (EPA), the Groundwater Protection Council, and independent agencies have found no evidence of groundwater contamination. In May 2011, EPA administrator Lisa Jackson stated before the U.S. House Oversight and Government Reform Committee that "I am not aware of any proven case where the fracking process itself affected water although there are investigations ongoing." Three of those investigations are in Texas, Wyoming, and Pennsylvania, and thus far the EPA has found no evidence of contamination; in the case of Wyoming, however, the EPA published faulty data with speculative and heavily contested conclusions. In all three cases, the EPA ignored state regulators' management of the alleged problems. Although previous EPA analysis of hydraulic fracturing found the process to be safe, the EPA now plans to publish a full study on hydraulic fracturing and drinking water that ostensibly demonstrates lack of safety. Analysis of the EPA's "Plan to Study the Potential Impacts of Hydraulic Fracturing on Drinking Water Resources" by the nonprofit technology research and development organization Battelle highlighted a number of concerns, including cherry-picking of data, lack of peer review, poor quality control, and a lack of transparency.

Myth #2: *The chemicals used in the fracking process are foreign chemicals that industry hides from the public.*

Fact: *Fracking fluid, made primarily of sand and water, uses a small percentage of chemicals that have common household applications and are regulated by the state.*

The fluid used in hydraulic fracturing is 99.5 percent water and sand. The 0.5 percent of additives (typically between three and 12 different chemicals) depends on the composition of the shale formation that varies by region and by well. The combination of additives function to dissolve minerals, prevent bacteria growth and pipe corrosion, minimize friction, and keep the fractures open or propped up. All chemicals used in the fracking process have common applications from swimming pool cleaners and laundry detergents to cosmetics, and even ice cream. None of these chemicals is hidden from the public, and federal law stipulates that a company must provide detailed chemical information sheets to emergency personnel in case of an accident. While states that have hydraulic fracturing laws have their own stipulations for chemical disclosure, the U.S. Department of Energy, in collaboration with the Groundwater Protection Council and industry, created the website FracFocus.org. The site provides a full list of chemicals used in the fracking process and companies voluntarily disclose the chemical makeup for specific wells across the country. FracFocus allows users to search wells by operator, state, and county.

Myth #3: *Wastewater from hydraulic fracturing is dangerous and unregulated.*

Fact: *Companies dispose of, and recycle, wastewater using many different methods, all of which are compliant with existing federal and state laws.*

Companies typically use around 4 million gallons of water—what a golf course uses in one week—to fracture a well by using water from lakes, rivers, or municipal supplies. Much of that water remains in the ground; about 15 percent to 20 percent of the water returns to the surface by flowing back through the well. The flow-back water contains the chemicals used in the fracking process and can also collect other naturally harmful substances in the ground. This water is never used for drinking and the disposal is subject to federal and state regulations. States have different regulations for disposal, and companies employ a variety of methods including temporary storage of wastewater in steel tanks or contained pits. More companies are recycling or reusing the flow-back water because it makes both economic and environmental sense. Other disposal methods include storing wastewater underground in injection wells that states regulate individually, and the EPA regulates under the Safe Drinking Water Act. The de-

States with Hydraulic Fracturing Since 2005

■ Hydraulic Fracturing*

* After a review of multiple data sources, cases of fracking for oil and gas have been substantiated since 2005. Maryland currently has a de facto moratorium on hydraulic fracturing. New York has a de facto moratorium on "high-volume horizontal fracturing" (using greater than 300,000 gallons of water) but fracturing in vertical wells or using lower volumes remains permissible.

TAKEN FROM: Matthew Freely, "Do You Live in One of the 32 States That Has Been Fracked?," EcoWatch, January 18, 2013.

mand for wastewater disposal and recycling is creating opportunities for new companies with emerging technologies to treat wastewater.

There have been concerns, in Pennsylvania for instance, that treating wastewater at sewage treatment plants that discharge into rivers supplying drinking water would contaminate drinking water with radioactive material. But Pennsylvania's Department of Environmental Protection found levels of radioactivity well within federal and state standards.

Norm Zellers, manager of the Sunbury Generation treatment facility in Snyder County, Pennsylvania, emphasized that "[y]ou can have more radioactivity on a bunch of bananas in the store or on a granite countertop." Wastewater management is another aspect of the fracking process that has been well regulated by existing federal and state laws, and the increased demand for wastewater treatment has driven the process to be cleaner and cheaper.

Myth #4: *Fracking causes earthquakes.*

Fact: *The fracking process itself does not cause earthquakes; in rare instances, the use of underground injection wells (for storage) has caused earthquakes. Induced seismic activity from many underground energy activities is not a new phenomenon and has been closely monitored by the Department of Energy.*

After a series of small earthquakes—ranging from 2.1 to 4.0 on the Richter scale—in Ohio and Arkansas near oil and gas sites, many have raised concerns about future tremors resulting from hydraulic fracturing. But the fracking process itself did not cause these earthquakes. The use of injection wells, an efficient and cost-effective way to dispose of briny wastewater, produced the seismic activity. Instances of seismic activity are rare; out of 30,000 injection wells, there have only been eight events of induced seismic activity—none of which caused significant property damage or injury. Induced seismicity does not occur only from oil and gas extraction. A recent National Research Council study highlights the fact that geothermal activities (capturing and using heat stored in the earth's core) have caused relatively small earthquakes (some felt, some not) at more frequent rates from far fewer projects. The study also warns that continuously injecting carbon dioxide at high pressures (carbon capture and sequestration from coal plants) could induce earthquakes of higher magnitudes.

Seismic activity as a result of underground activity is also not a new phenomenon. The U.S. Department of Energy has been observing and monitoring induced seismic activity from energy-related activities since the 1930s. While companies that induce seismic activity should be liable for any damage they cause, calls for bans of hydraulic fracturing or the use of underground injection wells are unfounded.

State Regulation, Federal Redundancy

One of the reasons why hydraulic fracturing has been so successful in promoting oil and gas development, while maintaining a strong environmental record, is the state regulatory regime. States in which fracturing takes place each have comprehensive regulation that ensures that oil and gas companies operate safely and in an environmentally sensible manner, and administer fines and implement punitive measures to correct any wrongdoing. In November 2011, the EPA's Lisa Jackson acknowledged the states' role: "States are stepping up and doing a good job. It doesn't have to be EPA that regulates the 10,000 wells that might go in." But states are not just now stepping up—states have effectively regulated oil and gas production and hydraulic fracturing for decades. In Pennsylvania, fracking has been taking place since the 1960s with nearly 100,000 oil and gas wells fracked and no instances of contamination of groundwater. The same clean record is true for Ohio, where over 70,000 oil and gas wells have been fracked since the 1960s. The Interstate Oil and Gas Compact Commission has compiled statistics for all 50 states, each of which has a flawless record when it comes to fracking and groundwater protection. . . .

Despite the states' effectiveness in regulating hydraulic fracturing and despite Jackson's comments, the EPA is pursuing onerous and duplicative regulations with weak scientific support. Many activities of oil and gas production are already subject to a number of major federal regulations, including the Clean Air Act (emissions), the Clean Water Act (surface water discharge), the Safe Drinking Water Act (wastewater management), the Emergency Planning and Community Right-to-Know Act (chemical disclosure for emergency responders), and the National Environmental Policy Act (production on federal lands), among others.

While many of these statutes are in need of serious reform, the White House's recently proposed fracking rules are unneeded and duplicative. The Department of the Interior released a draft rule on public disclosure of chemicals on federal lands despite the fact that states have successfully managed chemical disclosure. Congress has also introduced legislation that would regulate fracking fluids under the Safe Drinking Water Act (SDWA) despite the fact that the 2005 Energy Policy Act codified that Congress never intended to regulate fracking (except when using diesel oil in the fracking process under SDWA). Hydraulic fracturing had been safely regulated for a quarter century before Congress even enacted SDWA in 1974.

In April 2012, the EPA announced its first air-emission rules for hydraulic fracturing. Rather than being aimed at fracking itself, this is a backdoor global warming regulation: The rule highlights the supposed environmental benefits of reducing emission of methane, a greenhouse gas. The EPA's rule miserably fails the cost-benefit test; the agency's own analysis projects $745 million in annual costs and just $11 million to $19 million in environmental benefits. Moreover, the EPA has grossly overestimated methane emissions from the wells. The rule also fails to quantify any benefits from reducing volatile organic compounds (VOC) and hazardous air pollutants (HAP). While the rule asserts that benefits exist, the draft also says that "with the data available, we [the EPA] are not able to provide credible health benefit estimates for the reduction in exposure to [hazardous air pollutants], ozone and [particulate matter] (2.5 microns and less) (PM2.5) for these rules."

Congress: Prevent Federal Overreach on Fracking

The states' effective regulation underscores the need for members of Congress to prevent federal intervention that would unnecessarily stall the oil and gas boom and drive up costs for producers (and thus consumers). The states with tremendous oil and natural gas reserves have the most to gain economically, and have the greatest incentive to protect their environments. States have qualified experts to handle the regulatory requirements surrounding hydraulic fracturing. To that end, Congress should:

- Prevent any federal agency from adding new regulations to hydraulic fracturing. The proposed federal regulations are unnecessary and duplicative.

- Prohibit federal regulators from using any statute to regulate greenhouse gas emissions. Greenhouse gas regulations would drive up the cost of energy for no meaningful change in the earth's temperature.

- Reaffirm the states' authority and effectiveness in regulating hydraulic fracturing. The states have effectively handled the disclosure of chemicals used in the fracking process and have effectively protected drinking water for decades.

Fracking: It's Important

Hydraulic fracturing and horizontal drilling should be celebrated as important technological progress that has opened new opportunities for the safe development of affordable, reliable energy. The facts and history of hydraulic fracturing indicate that many of the fears associated with the process are exaggerated or unsubstantiated. Entrepreneurs created an energy boom and state regulators have been ensuring that energy production occurs in an environmentally sensible way. Congress should keep it that way.

"The bottom line is that drilling permits have been systematically approved for thousands of wells based on response plans that are reliant on chemical solutions that are at worst, largely untested, and at best, toxic to the few marine animals on which they have been tested."

The Chemical Dispersants Used in Oil Spills Are Toxic

Jacqueline Savitz

Jacqueline Savitz is the senior campaign director of Oceana, a global ocean conservation organization. In the following viewpoint, she testifies that the chemical dispersants used to break up the oil from the Deepwater Horizon spill in the Gulf of Mexico further contaminated the ecosystem and will have serious long-term environmental and health effects on the region. Savitz contends that it is unacceptable that the only response to the oil spill was the use of chemical dispersants that were known to be harmful to the marine environment; if oil companies want to drill in the nation's waters, she argues, they should show that they have an effective and environmentally responsible disaster response plan before they are even granted a permit. Savitz suggests that

Jacqueline Savitz, Written Statement before the Hearing on the Use of Dispersant for the Deepwater Horizon BP Oil Spill, US Senate Committee on Environment and Public Works, August 4, 2010.

because of the frequency of oil spills all over the country, the terrible side effects of chemical dispersants, and the general inadequacy of disaster response to such incidents, offshore oil drilling cannot be done safely. It is time, she maintains, to redouble our efforts to switch to clean energy sources.

As you read, consider the following questions:

1. According to Savitz, how many deaths were directly caused by the Deepwater Horizon disaster?

2. How many gallons of oil does Savitz estimate were dumped into the Gulf of Mexico because of the Deepwater Horizon blowout?

3. What countries are the top two suppliers of foreign oil to the United States, according to Savitz?

In the past three months [April 20, 2010, to August 4, 2010], our nation has been shaken by an oil spill of unprecedented proportions. The Deepwater Horizon blowout and subsequent three months of oil flow rivals the worst accidental oil spills in world history. It has directly caused 11 deaths, and it has put an untold thousands of people out of work. It has shut down fisheries, and threatened businesses that depend on tourism in five states. While we are beginning to see the end of the spill itself, its impacts will continue, perhaps for decades.

Marine life affected by the spill ranges from the smallest marine zooplankton species which play an important role at the base of the food chain, to commercially important species of oysters, fish, crabs, and shrimp. It includes four endangered and one threatened species of sea turtles, as well as the prized Atlantic bluefin tuna, whose populations have been depleted by overfishing to about 10% of historic levels. One of only two spawning grounds on the planet for Atlantic bluefin tuna was marred during spawning season this year with a mixture of toxic oil and chemical dispersants at the exact time that the species tends to release its eggs. This habitat has continued to be contaminated through the hatching period and the most sensitive life stages of the Atlantic bluefin.

The blowout of the well occurred, and the spill continued, through a time period that is for many species a spawning, breeding, nesting and or hatching season. Oil, chemical dispersants, and drilling muds are all toxic to marine life. Some species are more sensitive than others; however, it is clear that larvae and juveniles of most species are the most sensitive life stages. For animals, such as sea turtles and bluefin tuna, which are already struggling to maintain their populations, the implications of this contaminated habitat could be devastating. Young may not survive long enough to bolster adult populations, and may not contribute reproductively as a result. For other species, the spill threatens to destroy habitats, deplete food sources, or otherwise shake up the balance of the ecosystem in ways that may have long-term and even detrimental effects.

The effects of the spill on these species or on the complex marine ecosystem as a whole may not be known for decades, and the full effects may never be clear. The thousands of birds that have been found dead are likely indicators of thousands more that were never found. The same is true for sea turtles, marine mammals, fish and invertebrates. Many animals affected by the spill won't be counted, some may drift about in the gulf and many will likely be scavenged by other animals. The effects on populations may be difficult to determine for a number of reasons. For example, baselines are not always available, it can be difficult to assess population sizes, and other stresses on the species may cloud an assessment of the impacts of the spill.

However, the devastation that is apparent, the lost lives, the livelihoods that have been destroyed, and the marine life that have been affected, while perhaps just the tip of the iceberg, gives a clear indication that the benefits of offshore drilling do not justify the risks.

The remainder of this [viewpoint] focuses on the following points:

- There is no way to create an effective response plan for a major oil spill.

- Dispersant use is a lose-lose proposition.

- Offshore drilling cannot be done safely.

- We can make offshore drilling unnecessary.

- We can protect the oceans from oil while also improving the economy.

An Effective Response Plan

There is no way to create an effective response plan for a major oil spill. Once a blowout or other spill occurs, there are few if any effective solutions. Those that have been proposed and tried are not very effective. Only a small percentage of the oil that reaches the ocean waters can be recovered. And techniques such as burns, dispersant chemicals, barrier islands and booms are either ineffective, or have major downsides, or both. The only effective way to prevent the devastation that follows an oil spill is to respond before it happens, and prevent it from occurring in the first place. Since this spill has shown so clearly that response capabilities are inadequate, the only sure way to prevent marine and other impacts is to say "no" to offshore drilling in the first place.

Dispersant Use Is a Lose-Lose Proposition

One lesson learned from the Deepwater Horizon disaster is that if drilling must proceed, at the very least there need to be effective oil spill response plans, devised *a priori*, before the drill hits the earth's crust, not as part of the response process itself.

If the government insists on granting permits to drill, that permission should be conditioned on a demonstration that the companies asking for the rights to drill offshore have the capacity to prevent a spill, to contain a spill and to clean up a spill. None of these requirements were met in the case of the Deepwater Horizon permit, and it appears that the same is true for many ongoing offshore drilling operations, and planned drilling projects. This is unacceptable.

An effective response plan should not include activities that, in themselves, are harmful to the marine environment. The use of dispersant chemicals is perhaps the best example of this; however, on-site burns and the burning off of oil and gas collected, as was done in the Deepwater Horizon disaster are also examples of response activities that impact the marine environment. Each of these activities also has public health implications. In spite of the fact that they are not effective and that they cause collateral damage to marine life, these activities have, in the past, been considered sufficient to make up a response plan.

However, response activities that require further contamination of the water column, or that result in the release of undetermined amounts of air pollution such as particulate matter, carbon dioxide, and sulfur and nitrogen oxides, for example, is not a solution, it's just another piece of the original problem.

This is clearly the case with chemical dispersants. Dispersants do have an upside. If applied within 24 hours of the spill, they are effective at dissolving the oil and removing it from the surface, where it is otherwise a threat to diving birds, surfacing marine mammals and sea turtles. In doing so, they prevent some of the oil from reaching land, where it would wash up on beaches and marshes and pose risks to public health.

Exposure to Marine Life

However, their use results in more oil being dissolved into the water column where fish and other marine life are continually exposed to it. As a result, dispersants increase the time period in which aquatic life is exposed as well as the areal extent of exposure in the water column. Because toxicity is a function of dose and time period of exposure, this increases the number of aquatic animals that are subjected to toxic conditions as well the degree of toxicity.

In addition to making the oil more available to marine life, dispersants themselves can be toxic to marine life, depending on the concentration. Moreover, the dispersant oil mixture can be more toxic than either of the two chemical mixtures alone, and in some cases their toxicity is synergistic, meaning that it is greater than the additive toxicity of the two mixtures. Furthermore, once the dispersant is mixed with oil, especially at depth, it is no longer possible to skim the oil or to collect any meaningful amount of it.

Oil, dispersants, and their mixture can have a wide variety of both acute and chronic effects on marine life. Some exposure can be lethal, but for those animals that survive it, these chemicals can affect reproduction, growth, disease resistance, digestion, and a long list of other essential life processes. However, little is known about the toxicity of dispersants, including those that have been preapproved for use by the Environmental Protection Agency. These chemicals have been tested on only a small subset of species, not necessarily inclusive of the most sensitive in a given drilling area. For example, data are not available on the full effects of these chemicals on the deepwater corals present near the drill site. These may be among the most sensitive species exposed to the chemicals, and they are slow growing. If affected by the chemical exposure, it will take many years for them to recover.

The bottom line is that drilling permits have been systematically approved for thousands of wells based on response plans that are reliant on chemical solutions that are at worst, largely untested, and at best, toxic to the few marine animals on which they have been tested. Rather than providing an adequate response, this guarantees that there will be environmental impacts on marine life in the case of an oil spill, and spills are unfortunately much more common that one might think.

Offshore Drilling Cannot Be Done Safely

Despite claims from many supporters of the industry, spills happen frequently, and not just from tankers. After the Montara spill, in 2009, a blowout in shallow water off the coast of Australia, which took more than two months to contain, it was clear that this could happen again and that it could happen in the United States. The technology being used in that case was not old-fashioned. It was the newest technology, the kind that many have argued is as safe and could not result in a spill. But it did result in the Australian spill, and about a year later, the newest technology again failed to prevent the devastating spill in the Gulf of Mexico.

Offshore drilling is a dangerous and dirty business. Besides the 11 lives and the 100 to 200 million gallons spilled in this case, the United States Minerals Management Service reports that there have been at least 21 offshore rig blowouts, 513 fires or explosions offshore and 30 fatalities from offshore oil and gas activities in the Gulf of Mexico since 2006.

Given what we now know about the inadequacy of spill response, the side effects of dispersant chemicals, and the frequency of spills, we would be remiss not to determine exactly how we replace our oil demand with clean energy.

Make Offshore Drilling Unnecessary

Additional offshore oil drilling will not lower gas prices, and it will put many jobs at risk. In 2009, the United States Department of Energy (DOE) estimated that by 2030 gasoline prices would be $3.88 per gallon if all the U.S. oceans were open for drilling—that's just three pennies less than if previously protected ocean areas remained closed.

Oil is a global commodity, therefore, additional U.S. oil supply from additional offshore oil drilling would have to be significant enough to alter the global price of oil in order to impact local gasoline prices. The United States simply cannot produce enough oil from the limited resource in its offshore areas to make a difference on global oil prices. Yet at the same time, as we have seen, an oil spill can threaten the livelihoods of thousands of fishermen as well as those in the restaurant, hotel and other industries who rely on coastal tourism.

The only way to become truly energy independent is to end our addiction to oil and begin relying instead on clean energy. The United States Department of Energy (DOE) estimates that even if we opened all of the offshore areas to drilling, the U.S. would still import about 58% of its oil supply. Currently, about 62% of the crude oil supplied to the United States comes from foreign sources, with the top two suppliers being Canada and Mexico. Importing more than half of our oil will not allow us to be energy independent, yet that is the best case scenario, even if we develop all of our offshore reserves.

Reducing Dependence on Foreign Oil

The United States simply does not have enough domestic oil to reduce its dependence on imports, much less to fulfill its demand. The best way to eliminate foreign oil dependence is to eliminate dependence on oil itself by developing alternative sources, rapidly switching to plug-in and electric vehicles and phasing out oil consumption in other portions of our economy like home heating and electricity generation.

Preliminary analysis by Oceana has demonstrated that the economically recoverable oil and gas on the Atlantic coast would provide less energy, for a greater cost and create fewer jobs than if the same resources were invested in developing offshore wind. Because offshore wind development is competitive with offshore oil for installation vessels, maritime expertise and other needs, developing both would be economically inefficient. This suggests that expanding drilling in the

Gulf of Mexico Oil Spill

On 22 April 2010, fires from an explosion two days earlier sank the Deepwater Horizon oil rig located in the Gulf of Mexico about 84 kilometers (52 miles) southeast of the coastal city and port of Venice, Louisiana. The deadly oil-well blowout created a massive oil spill from a deepwater well located 1500 meters (5,000 feet) below the surface that ultimately became the worst accidental marine oil spill in history. The spill continued for 87 days, closing a significant portion of the gulf to fishing and fouled approximately 600 miles of coastline, washing oil into marshes, wetlands, and inland waterways. The spill delivered a crippling blow to the economic base of the region, disrupting lives and livelihoods along the central and northern Gulf coast. The spill and cleanup efforts killed thousands of birds and marine animals, imperiling both local and migratory species.

"Gulf of Mexico Spill,"
Global Issues in Context Online Collections 2014.

Atlantic is unnecessary and, in fact, counterproductive to the development of a clean energy economy.

Only 8% of the oil used in the United States comes from the Gulf of Mexico. This amount could be replaced by a combination of 1) increasing efficiency of home heating by shifting some oil heated homes to electric heat; 2) electrification of a portion of the U.S. vehicle fleet; 3) slowing ships to increase fuel efficiency and save costs; 4) shifting the small amount of oil-driven power generation to clean power, such as offshore wind; and 5) carefully increasing the use of advanced biofuels that come from non-food crops, prioritizing those with minimized energy costs. If we also begin to feed the electric grid with clean energy, from offshore wind, for example, these additional electricity demands will not have to be met by fossil fuels.

These steps could allow the U.S. to stop offshore drilling without increasing imports. If developed further, they ultimately could also alleviate the need for imports from countries that are not U.S. allies.

Because there are clear options that, if developed, could allow us to accelerate our shift to a clean energy economy, we believe that a Blue Ribbon Panel of experts should be appointed and charged with developing a plan to make these changes as soon as possible. While the president's [National Commission on the] BP Deepwater Horizon Oil Spill and Offshore Drilling is not charged with recommending alternatives to offshore drilling, the impacts of the Deepwater Horizon clearly demand that we ask these questions and find a way to break our oil habit. We should have the brightest minds in the U.S. engaged to develop a plan to fast track the shift to clean energy.

Protect the Oceans from Oil While Also Improving the Economy

The subject of this hearing is the use of dispersant chemicals in the Deepwater Horizon oil spill. The decision to use dispersants is perhaps the best example of the many "lesser of two evils" decisions that have had to be made as a result of the Deepwater Horizon spill. This call had to be made without the benefit of a crystal ball. There is no calculus to allow scientists to compare the ecological benefits of dispersant use to its ecological costs, and come out with the "right" answer for the oceans. The decision is a trade-off between surface oil slicks and oiled shorelines, versus oil and dispersants in the water column. The result of the decision to use dispersants is more oil and dispersants in the water column and more exposure to fish and invertebrates that live in the oceans.

This decision required the oceans and marine life to "take one for the team." The full effects of these actions may not be known for some time, if ever. However, it is important to recognize that this was not a "solution" or an "effective response." Rather it was a major detriment to our oceans, an insult following an already damaging injury.

The use of dispersants was just one of the "lesser of two evils" choices that result in harm to our oceans. There was the debate over burning oil off the water surface, or not burning it and the concerns about burning off the collected oil and gas because of the inherent and unmitigated air pollution it creates. There was the question of whether after the well was capped, whether the cap may need to be removed if there was a leak in the pipe which would mean more gushing oil into the ocean, to prevent a worse situation from developing around a new lead that may be identified. There has been a debate about the impacts of building barrier islands to stop oil flow into the marshes. There are concerns about the impacts to the marshes from all the additional activities needed for spill response. The oceans and marine ecosystems have suffered from more than just an oil spill. They have borne the brunt of many lose-lose choices that were necessary once the oil hit the water.

If we are going to have to ask the oceans to "take one, or many, for the team" we should, in response, take all necessary measures to make sure the situation is not repeated. That means making sure there are no more oil spills, and no more situations where dispersant chemicals are considered the best option. Since the drilling process has been so clearly shown to be unsafe, unpredictable and damaging, the only way to effectively prevent this type of spill and the consequent additional impacts, is to stop offshore drilling.

Recommendations

With the potential to develop clean energy solutions that could reduce our need for oil, create jobs and build our economy, the prospect of ending offshore drilling could lead to major benefits. Doing so could reduce and ultimately end the need for debate over dispersants, and other "lesser of two evil" decisions. Oceana therefore makes the following recommendations:

Stop Offshore Drilling

We have learned from the Deepwater Horizon disaster that we are not prepared to respond to an oil spill. Techniques that have been promised in response plans have proven ineffective, and often, as in the case of chemical dispersants, are used only at the expense of the marine ecosystem. The insufficient response capabilities, combined with the inability to prevent spills and to fully restore ecosystems to pre-spill conditions justify a permanent ban on offshore drilling.

Stimulate Clean Energy Solutions

By stimulating clean energy solutions, such as solar power, onshore and offshore wind energy, geothermal energy and energy efficiency, we can replace the oil we would obtain from the Gulf of Mexico, and then some. In doing so, we could alleviate the risks of offshore drilling while also strengthening the U.S. position in clean energy technology. One part of this should include stimulating the development of a clean energy manufacturing base in the Gulf region to allow a transition of oil and gas workers to clean energy jobs. Developing these clean technologies and manufacturing the needed components in the U.S. would allow us to reduce imports and increase exports.

Appoint a Blue Ribbon Solutions Commission

A Blue Ribbon Panel of experts should be appointed and charged with developing a plan to fast track the shift to clean energy. While the president's [National Commission on the]

BP Deepwater Horizon Oil Spill and Offshore Drilling is not charged with recommending alternatives to offshore drilling, the impacts of the Deepwater Horizon clearly demand that we ask these questions and find a way to break our oil habit.

> "Spill response often involves a series of
> environmental trade-offs."

The Use of Chemical Dispersants to Treat Oil Spills Involves Environmental Trade-Offs

David Westerholm

David Westerholm is the director of the Office of Response and Restoration, National Ocean Service, National Oceanic and Atmospheric Administration (NOAA). In the following viewpoint, he maintains that there is no perfect response to major oil spills such as the 2010 Deepwater Horizon disaster. In such cases, authorities must often sort through imperfect options in a very short amount of time and make the best decision possible to minimize the overall environmental damage. While chemical dispersants do not remove the oil from the water, they do speed up the degradation of the oil and reduce the amount of oil on the surface, where it could adversely affect birds, mammals, and turtles. It is essential in such situations to prevent the oil from reaching the shoreline and destroying vital marshes, fish and bird habitats, fisheries, and beaches. Unfortunately, the trade-off

David Westerholm, Written Statement before the Hearing on the Use of Dispersant for the Deepwater Horizon BP Oil Spill, US Senate Committee on Environment and Public Works, August 4, 2010.

is that chemical dispersants could do long-term damage to aquatic life and delicate marine ecosystems. In Westerholm's opinion, the use of chemical dispersants was the best option available to mitigate the shoreline impacts along the coast from the Deepwater Horizon spill.

As you read, consider the following questions:

1. According to Westerholm, under what federal act is the US Environmental Protection Agency (EPA) required to prepare and maintain a schedule of dispersants and other mitigating devices and substances in case of an oil spill?

2. How many million gallons of dispersants does Westerholm report were used in the Deepwater Horizon oil spill?

3. Under ideal conditions, how many gallons of oil are prevented from coming to the shoreline because of the use of one gallon of chemical dispersant, according to Westerholm?

The Deepwater Horizon BP oil spill is a stark reminder that large oil spills still occur, and that we must rebuild and maintain our response capacity. When an oil spill occurs, there are no good outcomes. Once oil has spilled, responders use a variety of oil spill countermeasures to reduce the adverse effects of spilled oil on the environment. The goal of the Unified Command is to minimize the environmental damage and speed recovery of injured resources. The overall response strategy to accomplish this goal is to maximize recovery and removal of the oil being released while minimizing any collateral damage that might be caused by the response itself. This philosophy involves making difficult decisions, often seeking the best way forward among imperfect options.

Under section 311 of the Clean Water Act, the U.S. Environmental Protection Agency (EPA) is required to prepare and maintain a schedule of dispersants and other mitigating devices and substances that may be used in carrying out the NCP [National Contingency Plan]. The NCP requires regional response teams (RRT), in which NOAA [National Oceanic and Atmospheric Administration] participates, and area committees to plan in the advance of spills for the use or non-use of dispersants, to ensure that the trade-off decisions between water column and surface/shoreline impacts are deliberated. As the FOSC [federal on-scene coordinator] for this spill response, the U.S. Coast Guard is responsible for approving the use of the specific dispersant used from the NCP product schedule. Because of the unprecedented nature of the dispersant operations, the monitoring and constraints on application volumes and methodologies are being closely managed. In particular, EPA has specified effectiveness and impact monitoring plans, application parameters, and action thresholds. Any changes to specific Deepwater Horizon dispersant plans require the concurrence of EPA and other RRT decision agencies, including NOAA, under the NCP.

NOAA's scientific support team is designated as a special team in the NCP and provides a broad array of scientific services to the response, including recommendations to the FOSC on the appropriate use of dispersants. NOAA is also a member of the Special Monitoring of Applied Response Technologies (SMART) program, an interagency, cooperatively designed program to monitor the efficacy of dispersant and *in situ* burning operations. SMART relies on small, highly mobile teams that collect real-time data using portable, rugged, and easy-to-use instruments during dispersant and *in situ* burning operations. Data are channeled to the Unified Command to help address critical questions. NOAA also uses SMART data to inform 24, 48 and 72 hour oil fate and trajectory models as dispersants can augment the behavior of the spilled oil.

The Gulf of Mexico shorelines, and Louisiana's in particular, possess extensive marsh habitats that are critical for wildlife and fisheries and shoreline protection. NOAA's environmental sensitivity index maps rank shoreline vulnerability to oil spills, and marshes are considered the most sensitive. Louisiana's marshes are already in a weakened condition and large areas are lost every year. These marshes and biota are extremely sensitive to oil, very difficult to clean up, and highly vulnerable to collateral impacts from response efforts.

The Response

For the Deepwater Horizon BP oil spill, the Unified Command's response posture has been to fight the spill offshore and reduce the amount of oil that comes ashore, using a variety of countermeasures including subsurface recovery, booming, skimming, burning, and dispersants. No single response method is 100 percent effective, and each has its own "window of opportunity" defined by the density and state of the oil and weather and sea state conditions, thereby establishing a need to consider the use of all available methods. Given the size and complexity of the Deepwater Horizon BP oil spill, no combination of response actions can fully contain the oil or completely mitigate the impacts until the well is brought under control. But given the enormous volume and geographic extent of the spill, the response to date has been successful in limiting shoreline impacts.

Chemical dispersants can be an effective tool in the response strategy, but like all methods, involve trade-offs in terms of effectiveness and potential for collateral impacts. Although mechanical recovery using skimmers is the preferred method of offshore oil spill response because it removes the oil from the environment, it is generally ineffective unless seas are fairly calm. The use of dispersants to mitigate offshore oil spills is a proven and accepted technology to reduce the impacts to shorelines and, under certain conditions, can be more effective than mechanical response. This is largely due to the fact that spray aircraft can encounter much more of the floating oil, and more quickly, than can skimmers. Dispersants have been used effectively to respond to spills both in the U.S. and internationally. In the U.S., notably in the Gulf of Mexico, dispersants have been used during the past 15 years against much smaller spills off Louisiana and Texas. The largest use of dispersants in North America (2.7 million gallons) was in the Gulf of Mexico during the 1979–80 Ixtoc I blowout in Campeche Bay, Mexico. The Deepwater Horizon BP oil spill response used about 1.8 million gallons of dispersant.

Assessing the Response for the Deepwater Horizon Disaster

The NCP establishes a framework for the use of dispersants in an oil spill response. The NCP states that RRT and area committees will address, as part of their planning activities, the desirability of using dispersants and oil spill control agents listed on the NCP's national product schedule. The NCP goes on to state that area contingency plans (ACP) will include applicable pre-authorization plans and address the specific contexts in which such products should and should not be used. If the RRT representatives for EPA, the Department of Commerce, and Department of the Interior natural resource trustees, and the states with jurisdiction over the regional waters for which the pre-authorization plan applies, approve in advance the use of certain dispersant products under specified circumstances as described in the pre-authorization plan, the FOSC may authorize the use of the products without obtaining additional concurrences. In Region VI, which includes the Gulf of Mexico, dispersant use is pre-authorized in offshore water, beyond the 3-mile limit. The pre-authorization of alternative countermeasures in the response plans allows for quick implementation of the pre-approved countermeasures during a response, when timely action is critical to mitigate environmental impacts.

For all dispersant operations, the FOSC must activate the SMART monitoring team to monitor the effectiveness of the dispersant. Dispersant use for the Deepwater Horizon BP oil spill was performed in accordance with ACP guidelines and with RRT approval. In consideration of the size and duration of the oil spill, the amounts of dispersant being used, and the uncommon sea bed injection method of application, a directive was approved by EPA and state representatives for the Region VI regional response team to put specific restrictions and monitoring requirements in place concerning dispersant use for the Deepwater Horizon BP oil spill as a condition of FOSC authorization for use. NOAA's scientific support coordinators, supported by NOAA's team of scientists and in consultation with trustees, is advising the FOSC on when and where dispersants should be used to determine the most effective and appropriate use of dispersants.

Chemical Dispersants

Dispersants are chemicals that may be applied directly to the spilled oil in order to remove it from the water surface by dispersing it into the upper layer of the water column. Dispersants are commonly applied through specialized equipment mounted on an airplane, helicopter or ship. The dispersant must be applied as a mist of fine droplets and under a specific range of wind and sea state conditions. Once applied at the surface, dispersants help break up the oil into tiny droplets (20–100 microns across; a micron is the size of the cross section of a hair) which mix into the upper layer of the ocean. Because of the high encounter rate of aircraft, they allow for the rapid treatment of large areas. Dispersed oil does not sink; rather it forms a "plume" or "cloud" of oil droplets just below the water surface. The dispersed oil mixes vertically and horizontally into the water column and is diluted. Once formed, bacteria and other microscopic organisms then act to degrade the oil within the droplets more quickly than if the oil had not been chemically dispersed. It should be noted that oil spilled from the Deepwater Horizon BP oil spill is also naturally dispersing into the water column due to the physical agitation of the wind, waves, and vessel operations.

During the first few months of the Deepwater Horizon BP oil spill, subsurface dispersants were applied directly at the well head where oil was being released through the use of remotely operated vehicles (ROV). The decision to use subsurface applications was made by the FOSC with concurrence by RRT Region VI after several test applications to determine the efficacy and development and implementation of a monitoring protocol. Monitored levels of dissolved oxygen levels within the dispersed oil plume and rotifer toxicity test results were reviewed daily to determine whether changes in the sea bed injection protocol should be considered. While there has been virtually no dispersant use since the well was capped on July 15 [2010], BP is continuing its environmental monitoring, under an EPA directive.

An Environmental Trade-Off

Spill response often involves a series of environmental trade-offs. The overall goal is to use the response tools and techniques that will minimize the overall environmental damage from the oil. The use of dispersants is an environmental trade-off between impacts within the water column, on the sea surface (birds, mammals, and turtles in slicks) and on the shore. Dispersants do not remove the oil from the environment, but it does speed up biodegradation of the oil. When a decision is made to use dispersants, the decision maker is reducing the amount of oil on the surface where it may affect birds, mammals and turtles, when they are at or near the surface, and ultimately that oil that may come ashore, in exchange for increasing the amount of oil in the upper layer of the water column 40 miles offshore. While the effects of dispersants on some water column biota have been studied, the effects of dispersants and dispersed oil below the surface on wildlife such as diving birds, marine mammals, and sea turtles are unknown. Under ideal conditions, each gallon of dispersant applied offshore prevents about 20 gallons of oil from coming onto the beaches and into the marshes of the Gulf coast.

The Gulf coast is home to coastal wetlands and marshes that are biologically productive and ecologically important to nesting waterfowl, sea turtles, fisheries, and essential fish habitat. The Gulf of Mexico region's ecological communities are essential to sustaining local economies, recreational experiences, and overall quality of life. The extensive marshes themselves provide coastal communities with protection from severe storms, such as Hurricane Katrina. These habitats are highly sensitive to oiling. Once oil does impact marshes, there are limited cleanup options and the potential for significant long-term impacts. As oil has moved ashore from the Louisiana coast to the Florida panhandle from the Deepwater Horizon BP oil spill, we have seen firsthand the impacts this oil has on these habitats, and to birds, turtles and other wildlife. Although it may not be readily apparent, use of dispersants offshore and in deep water, is reducing the amount of oil reaching the shoreline, reducing the amount of shoreline cleanup that will be required, and helping to reduce recovery time of injured near-shore resources. Without the use of dispersants, the shoreline impacts along the Gulf coast from the Deepwater Horizon BP oil spill would be greater.

Periodical and Internet Sources Bibliography

The following articles have been selected to supplement the diverse views presented in this chapter.

Kevin Begos	"4 States Confirm Water Pollution from Drilling," *USA Today*, January 5, 2014.
David Biello	"Hydraulic Fracturing for Natural Gas Pollutes Water Wells," *Scientific American*, May 9, 2011.
Eric Chemi	"Forget West Virginia. Chemical Spills Are an American Tradition," *Bloomberg Businessweek*, January 22, 2014.
Jordan Howard	"Fracking Pros and Cons: Weighing In on Hydraulic Fracturing," *Huffington Post*, November 10, 2011.
Ethan A. Huff	"Strontium, PFOA, and Toxic Chemicals Found in One-Third of U.S. Water Supply," *Natural News*, December 29, 2013.
Michael B. Kelley	"The 10 Scariest Chemicals Used in Hydraulic Fracking," *Business Insider*, March 16, 2012.
Michael B. McElroy and Xi Lu	"Fracking's Future: Natural Gas, the Economy, and America's Energy Prospects," *Harvard Magazine*, January–February 2013.
Brad Plumer	"Five Big Questions About the Massive Chemical Spill in West Virginia," *Washington Post*, January 21, 2014.
Richard Thompson	"4 Years After Spill Questions Remain About Health Impacts," *Advocate* (Baton Rouge, LA), May 17, 2014.
Julia Whitty	"Chemical Dispersant Made BP Oilspill 52 Times More Toxic," *Mother Jones*, December 4, 2012.

CHAPTER 4

How Should the Government Protect Americans from Toxic Chemicals?

Chapter Preface

Around 7:30 P.M. on April 17, 2013, local firefighters were called to a fire at the West Fertilizer Company, a storage and distribution facility in the town of West, Texas. Founded in 1962, the company stored large amounts of chemicals and distributed them to farmers for use as fertilizer. At the time of the fire, the facility had on hand a stockpile of 270 tons of ammonium nitrate, a high-nitrogen fertilizer commonly used in agricultural production. As the firefighters were setting up on site, a violent explosion ripped through the plant and surrounding area, killing eleven firefighters and four civilians.

Many people in the area later reported that the devastating blast felt like an earthquake; it actually registered on seismographs as a 2.1 quake and was felt as far as fifty miles away. It was so powerful that it also destroyed homes and severely damaged the West Middle School, which was located next door to the chemical storage facility. Later reports estimated that more than two hundred people were injured.

In the months after the disaster, several state and federal agencies began to investigate the circumstances leading up to the explosion. On May 7, the State Fire Marshal's Office of Texas determined that the facility's large stockpile of ammonium nitrate was the cause of the violent blast, which detonated when the fire reached the chemical storage area. Ammonium nitrate is highly combustible under certain conditions and was used as an ingredient in the 1995 bombing of the Alfred P. Murrah Federal Building in Oklahoma City, Oklahoma, which killed 168 people.

Another area of investigation centered on the role of federal and state oversight of the chemical storage and distribution plant. According to regulations, the company had filed a risk management plan with the Environmental Protection Agency (EPA) in 2011, but it had listed only the anhydrous ammonia it had stored at the facility—not the large stockpiles of ammonium nitrate that caused the explosion in 2013. Also, it never had filed a legally required report with the US Department of Homeland Security (DHS) stating that it had a large amount of hazardous fertilizer on the premises. State and local regulators were aware of the ammonium nitrate, however, and had found violations of storage procedures during past inspections.

Federal investigators concluded that a patchwork of federal, state, and local regulations allowed huge gaps in oversight, leading to the deadly disaster in West, Texas. They maintained that the chemical regulatory system was outdated and inefficient and required significant reforms. In the aftermath of the investigation, chemical safety experts pressed for a far more effective regulatory system to prevent further incidents like the one in West.

The storage and distribution of hazardous chemicals such as those that caused the West Fertilizer explosion in Texas is one of the topics explored in the following chapter, which examines the role of the federal government in protecting the American people from toxic chemicals. Other viewpoints in the chapter discuss how federal regulators should approach the movement to ban the controversial chemical bisphenol A (BPA) and the question of whether the government should pass updated and improved chemical safety legislation such as the Chemical Safety Improvement Act (CSIA).

"*If average citizens are to have any hope of a toxin-free lifestyle, we need the government to step in and regulate the poisonous substances that we are being exposed to on a daily basis.*"

A Truly Toxic Issue

Sadhbh Walshe

Sadhbh Walshe is a political commentator, writer, and filmmaker. In the following viewpoint, she is disconcerted by a 2010 report from the President's Cancer Panel that finds that Americans are bombarded daily with thousands of toxic chemicals—many of them unregulated—and that the risk of environmentally induced cancer has been severely underestimated by health authorities. The report also reveals that babies often are exposed to toxic chemicals while in the womb, which in high doses can lead to a variety of health and developmental problems. Walshe points out that the danger is not just from food; dangerous chemicals can be found in the things around us, including our furniture, food containers, vehicles, carpets, and plastic products. The federal government has a vital role in helping to protect the American public from these poisonous substances through effective legislation.

As you read, consider the following questions:

1. According to a 2010 report, how many chemicals are Americans using in their daily lives?

2. When does the author say that Canada banned bisphenol A (BPA)?

3. According to the President's Cancer Panel, what percentage of Americans will be diagnosed with cancer at some point in their lives?

I used to be under the impression that you had a reasonable chance of avoiding debilitating and potentially fatal diseases like cancer if you just took a few simple precautions: ate plenty of fruit and vegetables, gave up smoking, drank in moderation and did a bit of exercise. It's since become apparent that the world we live in is so overrun with environmental pollutants that it is next to impossible to keep oneself truly healthy.

A Troubling Report

A report released in the US earlier this year [2010] by the President's Cancer Panel concluded that the risk of environmentally induced cancer has been grossly underestimated; that exposure to potential carcinogens is widespread; that the 80,000 or so chemicals used by millions of Americans in their daily lives (mostly inadvertently) are largely unregulated and that, to a "disturbing extent", babies are being born "pre-polluted".

As someone who has spent a great deal of her time cycling around farmers' markets in inclement weather to fill cloth bags with local seasonal and organic produce, and sweating out toxins in hot yoga studios in between, these findings are particularly enraging.

I've known for a while that imbibing food is a perilous adventure. Meat, fish and dairy products have long since terrified me. Even fresh produce has its dangers. A conventional apple for example—the very fruit that is meant to keep the doctor at bay—can contain up to 42 different pesticides, many of them known carcinogens.

But now, it seems that food is the least of our worries, to the extent that you have some control over what you digest. The fact is we are being bombarded 24/7 by toxic chemicals: benzene and formaldehyde in our furniture and carpets, bisphenol A (BPA) in food containers and the coating on credit card receipts, and who knows what in our electronic devices.

BPA

Some of these chemicals, like formaldehyde (which is probably in the desk I'm typing at right now and in the sofa I'll be reclining on later) and BPA, which is everywhere, have been the subject of hundreds of studies and are known to be harmful, even in very low doses. BPA is particularly troubling, being linked to breast cancer, infertility and birth defects in infants (reducing the normal distance between their anus and genitals for example), yet it is ubiquitous in—of all things— babies' bottles. BPA was banned from use in Canada in 2008; despite more than 700 studies coming to the same distressing conclusion, it is still FDA [Food and Drug Administration]- approved for use in the United States.

And these are just the chemicals we know about. What damage the other 79,998 or so chemicals floating about are causing is anybody's guess.

A Toxin-Free Life

You can, of course, minimise your exposure to toxic chemicals by adhering to the following set of guidelines: buy food, home and garden products, toys, medicines, furniture and clothing that are organic and free of BPA, phthalates, endocrine disruptors, formaldehyde and other toxic by-products of the manufacturing process. Filter your water and air, don't use

© Ralph Hagen/CartoonStock.com.

your mobile phone, don't use Wi-Fi, don't use the microwave, steer clear of electronic devices generally, wear sunscreen, avoid carpets, test your house for mould, test your house for radon levels, avoid first-, second- and third-hand smoke—and next time you sign a credit card receipt, try not to touch it.

No problem, right? Well, not if you have the resources of someone like Madonna or Gwyneth Paltrow, perhaps, but for the average Joe, toxin-free living is simply not feasible. I can't get my landlord to clean the windows in my apartment—so there's no way he's checking the radon levels anytime soon. And how, exactly, is one supposed to recognise an endocrine disruptor when it comes knocking?

For people of limited means, this is an even bigger problem. They have enough to be getting on with trying to put food on the table without having to worry whether the food, not to mention the table itself, is safe.

The Role of Government

If average citizens are to have any hope of a toxin-free lifestyle, we need the government to step in and regulate the poisonous substances that we are being exposed to on a daily basis. Fortunately, there is some light at the end of the tunnel. Last April, Senator [Frank] Lautenberg proposed the Safe Chemicals Act, which would overhaul the dangerously outdated Toxic Substances Control Act of 1976. The new act, like many others before, is still waiting for congressional approval and you can be sure that the longer it languishes, the happier the plastics and manufacturing industries will be.

Meanwhile, according to the President's Cancer Panel, a whopping 41% of Americans—almost half the population—will be diagnosed with cancer at some point in their lives. In 2009 alone, 562,000 Americans died from the disease.

"When it comes to stories on so-called
toxic substances, the public discourse
seems infected by a malady worse than
microscopic residues: chemophobia."

The US Government Should Not Rush to Ban Chemicals

Jon Entine

*Jon Entine is an author, a journalist, the director of the Genetic
Literacy Project, and a resident scholar at the American Enterprise Institute. In the following viewpoint, he finds that there is a
pervasive chemophobia when it comes to so-called toxic chemicals that is based on exaggerated fears that some chemicals are
always harmful, even when the amount that humans are exposed to is so miniscule that there is virtually no danger of adverse health effects. Entine stresses that not all chemicals are bad;
very often, the toxicity of a certain chemical depends on the level
of exposure. He urges authorities to be cautious when it comes to
chemical bans, as many of these chemicals have essential uses
and banning effective chemicals has consequences. Entine concludes that the US government should not base policy on public
anxiety unless the trade-off is clear and significant.*

As you read, consider the following questions:

1. According to a Centers for Disease Control and Prevention (CDC) report, what percentage of Americans were found to have measurable amounts of bisphenol A (BPA) in their urine?

2. Why does the author think that the Environmental Protection Agency (EPA) is reviewing the limits on perchlorate?

3. How many chemicals does Entine identify as potentially banned under new guidelines in Europe?

The health-scare headline of the week: "Americans found to have twice as much bisphenol A [BPA] in their bodies as Canadians."

BPA, as it is known, is a widely used chemical found in baby bottles, containers, CDs, car dashboards and even in dental sealants. A new survey finds that Canadians on average have about 1 part per billion of BPA in their urine, while Americans have twice that amount.

"That's bad news for Americans," observes Mother Nature Network news. "Scientists are worried about BPA," writes the *Toronto Globe and Mail*.

But most scientists are not worried and do not see this survey as bad news. In fact, it's not news at all. Almost without exception, the hundreds of media outlets that have run with this story have failed to mention that regulatory scientists throughout the world have uniformly concluded that these levels of BPA are so miniscule as to be basically harmless.

"Finding a measurable amount of bisphenol A in the urine does not mean that [it] causes an adverse health effect," the Centers for Disease Control and Prevention [CDC] reported recently, noting that it is found in more than 90 percent of Americans but is "excreted in the urine within 24 hours with no evidence of accumulation."

Exposure vs. Effect

When it comes to stories on so-called toxic substances, the public discourse seems infected by a malady worse than microscopic residues: chemophobia. Webster's defines chemophobia as the irrational belief that "chemicals" are bad and "natural" things are good. Labeling a chemical "toxic" or a "contaminant" is meaningless. Toxicity is a question of degree; exposure is different from effect.

It's critical to examine the consequences of banning a particular chemical. Among its myriad uses, BPA can be found in can liners that increase the shelf life of food and prevent botulism, which is a genuine health threat. There are no effective substitutes. Ban BPA and people are likely to die.

Many activists claim that dental sealants made with BPA can act as a "hormone disruptor." The science says otherwise. According to a 2010 Harvard study, the one-time exposure to BPA that occurs when sealants are put in is only one-fifth to one-half the exposure a child faces daily from environmental sources. "We believe the high preventive benefits of sealants far outweigh the risk," concludes pediatric endocrinologist Abby Fleisch.

"Based on current research, the [American Dental Association] agrees with the authoritative government agencies that the low-level of BPA exposure that may result from dental sealants and composites poses no known health threat."

The FDA [US Food and Drug Administration], under President [Barack] Obama, has rejected calls to restrict the use of BPA, noting that its benefits outweigh its risks. When asked last year whether it was harmful to pregnant women or children, deputy commissioner Dr. Joshua Sharfstein didn't mince words: "If we thought it was unsafe, we would be taking strong regulatory action." Sharfstein's view is in line with international regulators. Not one science-based agency in the world has called for a ban of BPA. (It was restricted for some uses in

Canada—when bureaucrats overruled Health Canada's science advisory board, which concluded that there was not sufficient evidence to justify a ban.)

But you'd never know that reading one of the hottest books on the activist's bookshelf: *Legally Poisoned: How the Law Puts Us at Risk from Toxicants.* University of California, Riverside, philosophy professor Carl [F.] Cranor literally demonizes BPA and dozens of other chemicals that regulators, by weight of evidence analysis, have deemed both useful and safe as used.

But not Cranor. He argues that "molecules are harmful." The problem with this attractively simplistic thesis is that everything is made of molecules and chemicals. Apples, bananas, basil, broccoli, cabbage, citrus fruits, mushrooms, turnips, and many more foods contain naturally occurring chemicals that are toxic—they cause cancer at large lifelong doses in laboratory rodents. Tofu is more estrogenic than BPA.

Outbreak of Chemophobia

This distressingly familiar chemophobic narrative derives from the precautionary principle—the notion, popular in Europe, that a substance can be banned even absent hard data and a cause-effect relationship if it is perceived as potentially harmful. The precautionary notion is not a scientific standard. It is an attitude rather than the kind of clear-cut rule that generally forms the basis for regulation. In its most extreme applications, trade-offs are not considered, such as the harm that might be caused from restricting a particular technology or the potential danger of substituting an untested substance for a thoroughly evaluated one.

More than anything, this precautionary notion gives legislators and politically appointed regulators—some with a limited scientific IQ—the freedom to pick and choose which substances to restrict. And it threatens to replace the risk standard long used in the U.S. and in most of the world.

Risk describes the probability of genuine danger. The key is setting an appropriate threshold. Until now, regulators have been ultra-cautious, especially in America—establishing limits hundreds to thousands of times more restrictive than those suggested by studies on sensitive laboratory animals. Under long-standing international protocol, as long as a substance doesn't violate a data-defined threshold with a cushion in the tens or hundreds of thousands, it has been allowed onto the market.

But with recent advances in bioanalysis, scientists are now able to isolate a thimbleful of a liquid poured into Lake Erie. Our technology is so advanced that parts per trillion can often be identified in pure water used for liquid chromatography. Exploiting unscientific fears of trace levels of chemicals, activists are putting pressure on regulators to set thresholds of what can be measured not on what is potentially dangerous—without evidence that current standards are inadequate.

The FDA, EPA [Environmental Protection Agency] and USDA [US Department of Agriculture] have to evaluate hazard and risk when making decisions on what to restrict and at what level of usage. Recently, the EPA announced it is reviewing the limits on perchlorate. The chemical is valuable when used as a key component in rocket fuel or to treat thyroid disorders, but can have health impacts at very high levels of exposure—which is rare. In other words, it offers benefits and risks. Weighing them is what sensible regulation is all about. (Let's hope the government's recommendations are based on the evidence and not on fears.) But 'sensible balance' is not what some health and environmental campaigners advocate.

Crop Chemophobia

Consider the case of nuts. Many natural fungi produce mycotoxins that affect up to 25 percent of the world's nut supply. One of these, aflatoxin, can be a significant factor in causing cancer, and infects up to 15% of California's almond crop.

States Considering Toxic Chemicals Policies in 2014

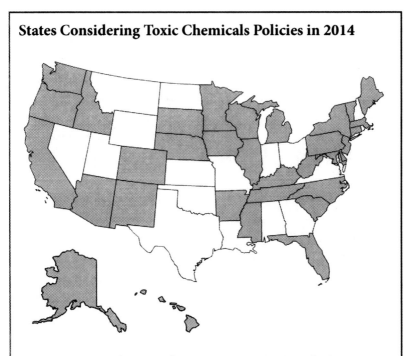

TAKEN FROM: Safer States, "At Least 33 States to Consider Toxics Policies in 2014," Coalition for a Safe and Healthy Connecticut, January 28, 2014.

The most effective and efficient containment strategy is to use insecticides to control insect crop pests, which would otherwise injure the nuts, seeds or grains, thus providing points of entry for the fungal pathogens to infect the mature or harvested crop and produce the toxins. Yet environmental campaigners adamantly oppose that method of control, in effect ignoring a natural toxic chemical while taking an inflexible stand against a synthetic protective chemical. Such trade-offs mean very real risks to consumers, which can result in injury and even serious illness, and some people may die.

They also have launched zealous campaigns against weed killers that are necessary for crops to flourish. For example, the common triazine herbicides, such as simazine and atrazine, have become central targets of anti-chemical campaigners. Yet, as one example, published studies show that legal limit on atrazine exposure has an extraordinary safety cushion—up to 1,000 times or more what advanced scientific studies have determined is safe for humans. But many environmental campaigners, citing controversial and contested studies on amphibians, lobby for a ban of triazines, atrazine in particular.

What do the frog studies show? Lab experiments by one prominent researcher who exposed clawed frogs to lower doses of atrazine produced males with ambiguous genitalia and squeaky, soprano-like croaks—hermaphrodites. University of California endocrinologist Tyrone Hayes labeled atrazine an "endocrine disruptor"—a term now used by chemical critics to stigmatize many chemicals not found to be carcinogenic.

Critics of atrazine have long contended that atrazine disrupts both the fertility and the normal sexual development of amphibians, which suggests potential danger to humans, particularly pregnant women or young children. But no studies actually show or even suggest that. Many plastics, as well as many natural substances such as clover, many fruits, and soy—together called phytoestrogens—subtly alter the way our hormones work. They key issue is: at what level of exposure.

Moreover, the EPA and the various independent scientists from around the world have doggedly tried to replicate Hayes's findings to no avail. Biologist Werner Kloas of Humboldt University of Berlin, who believes that chemicals should be banned for precautionary reasons if the evidence is ambiguous, found no impact on clawed frogs at concentrations comparable to those investigated by Hayes.

Most recently, David Skelly, professor of ecology at the Yale School of Forestry & Environmental Studies, who is a firm proponent of the "atrazine retards frogs" school, was flabbergasted to discover that the deformities he found in field studies were actually lowest in farmlands, where atrazine is often used, as compared to cities and suburbs—a direct challenge to the activist hypothesis.

"[W]e found that in those kinds of landscapes where corn is being grown, the great majority of the ponds we sampled didn't have any deformities at all."

Skelly's findings underscore one of the fundamental truths of science: Data and context are more important than ideology, however well motivated. Branding any chemical as a toxic "endocrine disruptor" is about as useful as describing a car as "fast." Terms such as "neurotoxic" or "endocrine disruptor" sound alarming, but they say nothing about how much of a substance might be problematic. Relative to what? Under what conditions in the real world? The question for regulators remains: What level of exposure to a substance causes a deleterious effect? As Paracelsus, the father of toxicology, observed, "All things are poison and nothing is without poison, only the dose permits something not to be poisonous."

Scientists at the World Health Organization [WHO], whose mandate is to protect the vulnerable, last year rejected calls by activists to ban atrazine. Recognizing its invaluable role in modern agriculture—atrazine significantly increases crop yields and lowers overall use of pesticides—and basing its decision on new health studies, WHO actually softened its limits to 100 parts per billion [ppb] in groundwater. Its new precautionary standard is now 33 times higher than the 3ppb in the U.S.

Health Trade-offs

WHO was wise to consider the trade-offs, because banning effective chemicals always has consequences. Agricultural chemicals are among the most scrutinized and regulated of all technologies. In Europe, which is already more restrictive than the U.S., governments are phasing in precautionary criteria that could blacklist 22 chemicals—about 15 percent of the E.U. [European Union] pesticide market. Some environmentalists are pressuring U.S. regulators to abandon a risk-based approach for this more politicized European standard. That would be a mistake.

The bottom line is that in order to maintain healthy crops, farmers fight a constant battle against insects, fungi and plant diseases, as well as weeds (which compete with crops for water, nutrients, and light). Advanced chemical technologies have helped to prevent infectious diseases and to enhance crop yields. These are the drivers of the Green Revolution, which has dramatically cut world hunger over the past 60 years.

Chemicals often get a bad rap. In the case of BPA, atrazine and other chemicals with demonstrable societal benefits, are we prepared to trade off the certainty that banning them will damage health against the long-shot possibility, based on contradictory studies on rodents or frogs, that a chemical might be harmful over a lifetime of exposure? That said, scientists must remain open to new evidence. We are developing sophisticated tools to evaluate exposure to chemicals, including examining their impacts on genes and hormonal systems. If the weight of evidence shifts, we have to be prepared to tighten regulations.

But acting precipitously based on public anxiety is a dangerous precedent. Bans make sense only if we gain identifiable health or environmental benefits in exchange. It's becoming increasingly difficult for the public to distinguish genuine risks from chemophobia. Advocacy groups and their enablers in the breathless media often compound the confusion. With the stakes so high, scientific literacy is no longer a luxury.

"*The U.S. needs to be a global leader in chemicals management, and to do that we need a robust national framework for chemicals regulation, one that is predictable and manageable for industry while increasing consumers' confidence that the chemicals used to make products are safe.*"

The Chemical Safety Improvement Act Should Be Passed

Linda Fisher

Linda Fisher is the vice president and chief sustainability officer for DuPont. In the following viewpoint, she urges the US Congress to pass the Chemical Safety Improvement Act, which would establish the nation as a leader in chemicals management programs. Such legislation is vital, she argues, because the existing law, the Toxic Substances Control Act of 1976, is outdated and ineffective. Fisher outlines the many benefits of modernizing the old law, including streamlining the ability of the Environmental Protection Agency (EPA) to assess existing chemicals and gather information on new ones; empowering the agency to efficiently act on dangerous chemicals to protect public health and the en-

Linda Fisher, "Strengthening Public Health Protections by Addressing Toxic Chemical Threats," US Senate Committee on Environment and Public Works, July 31, 2013.

vironment; and providing more transparency to the public on chemicals management. Although there are minor changes that could be made to improve the bill, she urges Congress to take the opportunity to pass the bill for the good of the industry and for consumers.

As you read, consider the following questions:

1. According to Fisher, in what year did REACH, the European product regulatory program, enter into force?

2. What does Fisher list as the first major change that needs to be made to the Toxic Substances Control Act?

3. What communities does Fisher cite as united in their support for the Chemical Safety Improvement Act?

Three years ago, I was asked to testify before this committee [U.S. Senate Committee on Environment and Public Works] on the need to modernize U.S. chemical management policies. I emphasized then that in the more than three decades since the Toxic Substances Control Act [TSCA] was signed into law, many things had changed rendering the statute outdated, especially in terms of how it treated existing chemicals. Scientific understanding and public awareness of exposure to chemicals have changed significantly since enactment. Countries around the world have adopted and are implementing strong new programs to regulate the manufacture and use of chemicals. Although significant attention is given to REACH [Registration, Evaluation, Authorisation and Restriction of Chemicals], the European product regulatory program which entered into force in 2007, since that time we have seen many regulatory programs springing up around the world in markets as diverse as Canada, China, Korea and Turkey.

And here at home, in the absence of federal legislation to reform TSCA, we continue to see an increasing number of actions by states to regulate chemicals. State-by-state chemical bans, restrictions, phaseouts and substitutions create tremendous uncertainty for businesses seeking to produce safe, reliable products that can be sold nationally and globally. In addition, consumers are demanding safer products and that is having an impact on the market value chain. Many of our customers are responding to consumer concerns about chemical safety by imposing restrictions on the use of certain chemicals in products. Some have called this "private regulation" and it imposes additional stress and uncertainty in the marketplace, as these private sector limitations seldom have the scientific rigor and transparency that a regulatory process provides.

Time to Reform the Toxic Substances Control Act

It is time to reform TSCA. The U.S. needs to be a global leader in chemicals management, and to do that we need a robust national framework for chemicals regulation, one that is predictable and manageable for industry while increasing consumers' confidence that the chemicals used to make products are safe. The Chemical Safety Improvement Act [CSIA] of 2013 gives us the vehicle to do just that.

I am personally, very grateful that the work begun under the late Senator [Frank] Lautenberg has continued under your leadership of the committee, Senator [Barbara] Boxer. TSCA is a very important statute, at times forgotten by the Congress, but one that is critical to public safety and to economic innovation in the U.S. I also want to express my appreciation for the work of Senator [David] Vitter, who with Senator Lautenberg introduced the Chemical Safety Improvement Act with a bipartisan group of cosponsors.

Over the years, considerable consensus has developed that several major changes to TSCA are needed in order to ensure that the U.S. has an effective chemical management regime going forward.

Essential Reforms

First, a modernized TSCA should require EPA to systematically assess existing chemicals. The statute's original drafters grandfathered existing substances and placed significant burdens on EPA before it could identify chemical risks and take action. This has generated public concern about whether we know enough about the chemicals that we are exposed to every day.

Second, data-gathering tools under TSCA should be less cumbersome and time consuming. A modernized TSCA should include a streamlined approach for EPA to gather the data they need. We believe that chemical producers and our value chain partners need to provide adequate data to allow EPA to assess the safety of chemicals in use and to develop suitable risk management approaches. EPA and companies should leverage existing data and data arising from other programs like REACH first, and then fill data gaps as necessary to complete assessments. For example, some nine thousand dossiers containing useful information have been submitted under REACH. Where more information is required we should strive to minimize animal testing where there are tools to get adequate data through other means.

Third, EPA's authorities to identify and act on chemicals that pose safety concerns should be streamlined. One of the biggest problems EPA faces in administering the current TSCA is the agency's inability to achieve timely risk reductions under Section 6 when faced with the need to reduce or eliminate exposures to a specific chemical. Although well intended by its drafters in 1976, the process under Section 6 has proven next to impossible for the agency to successfully implement.

Fourth, more data should be available to the public while respecting legitimate confidential business information (CBI). Maintaining industry's ability to preserve CBI and prevent piracy of intellectual property is critical to encouraging the kind of innovation that will lead to safer and safer chemical alternatives. I think everyone agrees that there are some straightforward means to improve the CBI process in ways that strike the right balance between the public's need for accurate information and the need to continue to incentivize innovation by American businesses.

Fifth, it is important that a modernized TSCA preserve the efficiency of the current PMN [premanufacturing notice] process for new chemicals. This is also critical to facilitating innovation, increasingly bringing green chemistry to market and allowing substitution where warranted.

Benefits of the Chemical Safety Improvement Act

The Chemical Safety Improvement Act effectively addresses each of these issues. First and perhaps most significantly, the Chemical Safety Improvement Act, if enacted, would for the first time direct EPA to systematically evaluate the safety of existing chemicals in use. This represents a significant and warranted change in federal chemical policy. No such requirement is present in the current TSCA.

Second, the bill streamlines EPA's authority to gather the data needed for the agency to determine whether a chemical is safe for its intended use, including additional testing. EPA's current authorities require extensive findings and rulemakings simply to gather data. First and foremost by requiring EPA to assess and affirmatively determine the safety of existing chemicals, the CSIA creates a powerful motivation for industry to voluntarily bring forward hazard and exposure data associated with their chemicals to ensure those assessments are as well informed as they can be. The CSIA also gives EPA a wide range of tools to collect information, including consent agreements, orders and rulemakings and removes the current requirement that EPA make a risk finding simply to ask for information.

What Would the Chemical Safety Improvement Act Do?

- Require Safety Evaluations for All Chemicals: All active chemicals in commerce must be evaluated for safety and labeled as either "high" or "low" priority chemical based on potential risk to human health and the environment. . . .

- Protect Public Health from Unsafe Chemicals: If a chemical is found to be unsafe, the Environmental Protection Agency [EPA] has the necessary authority to take action. . . .

- Prioritize Chemicals for Review: The Environmental Protection Agency will have to transparently assess risk, determine safety, and apply any needed measures to manage risks.

- Screen New Chemicals for Safety: New chemicals entering the market must be screened for safety and the EPA is given the authority to prohibit unsafe chemicals from entering the market. . . .

- Promote Innovation and Safer Chemistry: This legislation provides clear paths to getting new chemistry on the market and protects trade secrets and intellectual property from disclosure.

- Protect Children and Pregnant Women: The legislation requires EPA to evaluate the risks posed to particularly vulnerable populations, such as children and pregnant women, when evaluating the safety of a chemical—a provision not included in existing law. . . .

"Bipartisan Legislation Would Protect Americans from Risks Posed by Exposure to Chemicals," US Senate Committee on Environment and Public Works, May 22, 2013.

Third, the CSIA streamlines EPA's authorities to identify and act on chemicals that may pose safety concerns in their use. We support the separation of the safety assessment on high-priority substances from the risk management assessment and decisions. We believe the bill wisely leaves the current TSCA safety standard largely in place. The challenge to implementation of Section 6 was never the standard, rather it was encumbrances like the "least burdensome" requirement that have made Section 6 unmanageable. The bill addresses this by removing that requirement and provides clear authority for the agency to require a variety of risk management actions, from labeling to banning specific uses of a chemical. As the bill progresses it will be important to clarify and ensure that the provisions of the revised Section 6 avoid the sort of "paralysis by analysis" that has hindered EPA's implementation of the current law.

Fourth, the CSIA ensures that more data will be made available to the public while respecting legitimate confidential business information (CBI). Let me start by pointing out that CBI designation has nothing to do with what information EPA sees—it relates solely to what information is made public, a public that includes not only U.S. citizens and public interest groups but commercial competitors and foreign nations. We appreciate that a lot of thoughtful work has been done by all stakeholders to strike the right balance between the public availability of information and the protection of legitimate trade secrets that is so important to the U.S. innovation economy. Borrowing from Senator Lautenberg's Safe Chemicals Act, the CSIA helpfully clarifies those categories of information which can and cannot receive CBI protections. It raises the bar on the rigor of substantiations of CBI claims. And it expressly provides otherwise CBI information to key interested parties, such as state governments which demonstrate the ability to protect such data.

Time to Take Action

We understand that many important stakeholders believe this bill needs changes. We have some changes that we would also like to see and that we believe will improve the bill. It is my personal belief that many of these issues can be addressed while still preserving the design, structure and key provisions of CSIA. I hope all interested stakeholders recognize just how much progress this bill represents, and the tremendous opportunity we have to move TSCA reform forward in a bipartisan way this year using this bill as a vehicle.

Madame Chair, we have before us a unique opportunity to pass comprehensive reform of the U.S. chemicals management programs, and once again place the U.S. government in a leadership position on this important issue. Rarely does industry ask for EPA to be vested with more power, rarely do many members of the NGO [nongovernmental organizations] community, the labor community and industry come to Congress supporting an environmental regulatory bill. We do so because the Chemical Safety Improvement Act represents much-needed sweeping reform to an outdated and largely ineffective existing chemicals program. I urge you to seize this opportunity.

> *"Though the intent may be otherwise, as drafted the [Chemical Safety Improvement Act] practically invites litigation, delays action on most chemicals, continues to constrain the development of health and safety information, and allows critical information to be hidden from the public."*

The Chemical Safety Improvement Act Should Not Be Passed

Andy Igrejas

Andy Igrejas is the director of Safer Chemicals, Healthy Families. In the following viewpoint, he states that the Chemical Safety Improvement Act (CSIA) of 2013 does not make the necessary reforms to the US system of chemicals management to better protect public health and the environment. As it stands, the CSIA needs much broader and well-considered reforms to be as effective as it needs to be to meet today's challenges. Igrejas points to a number of problems with the proposed legislation, including that it forces unnecessary delays on chemical investigations; does not establish a clear, risk-based safety standard for chemicals; fails to streamline chemical testing requirements;

Andy Igrejas, "Testimony on the Chemical Safety Improvement Act (S. 10009)," US House of Representatives Energy and Commerce Committee, November 13, 2013.

complicates the right of states to develop their own chemical policies; and allows too much secrecy when it comes to key information about chemical safety. He recommends a significant reworking of the bill before it can be passed.

As you read, consider the following questions:

1. According to Igrejas, what key study from 1993 found that a failure to account for vulnerable populations meant that Environmental Protection Agency (EPA) decisions about pesticides did not protect children from exposure to the pesticide residues in food?

2. How many subsections in the Chemical Safety Improvement Act does Igrejas say are about the EPA developing new frameworks, policies, and guidance on scientific questions?

3. What four states does Igrejas identify as developing more comprehensive policies that address broader classes of chemicals than the Chemical Safety Improvement Act?

The focus of today's hearing is S. 1009, the Chemical Safety Improvement Act (CSIA). The Senate bill has raised hopes that reform can be enacted in this Congress. We share those hopes. At the same time, there are standards that any reform must meet to be credible and meaningful. As drafted, the CSIA does not meet those standards. We offer the following critique of the legislation in a constructive spirit with the hope that it can inform Congress's work.

In previous hearings the committee [US House of Representatives Energy and Commerce Committee] began the process of understanding what didn't work in TSCA [Toxic Substances Control Act] and why, and of identifying the critical fixes needed in any reform. Congress can craft a law that will enjoy broad support from the health and environmental community if it focuses tightly on the most critical elements to achieve the clearest possible protections for public health and the environment. I hope my testimony suggests a path forward.

Key Lessons of TSCA

As previous testimony has shown, TSCA failed for a variety of reasons. The standard in the bill proved impossible to meet. Unlike other environmental and public health laws, it was not a strictly risk-based or health-based standard. The standard bound up consideration of the risks of a chemical with the evaluation of its benefits and the costs of any proposed restrictions. The law also required EPA [Environmental Protection Agency] not merely to choose proportional risk management measures, but to demonstrate it had chosen the "least burdensome" of those measures. It made it difficult for EPA to require the development of health and safety information on a chemical. It allowed companies to claim information confidential without justification. It did not set clear deadlines or timelines for EPA action. Its procedures were cumbersome and some of its terminology vague, leading to fatal delays and litigation. In retrospect, TSCA's only clear achievement was the ban on PCBs [polychlorinated biphenyls, a toxic chemical used in electronics and manufacturing] and its saving grace was that it did not unduly restrict the states. In the 36 years of federal dysfunction the states have stepped forward to fill the gap.

The fundamental problem with the CSIA is that it fails to learn from these lessons. Though the intent may be otherwise, as drafted the CSIA practically invites litigation, delays action on most chemicals, continues to constrain the development of health and safety information, and allows critical information to be hidden from the public. But this time it would also restrict the states even in the absence of meaningful action from the federal government.

The Safety Standard

A core idea of the CSIA is that it "fixes" TSCA's standard rather than imposing a new standard such as "reasonable certainty of no harm" as proposed in previous reform legislation. At its most basic level, fixing the standard means changing it to be a risk-based standard, rather than one that balances the risks and benefits and also requires EPA to choose the "least burdensome" regulatory approach. It is the commingling of these considerations that the court cited in blocking EPA from regulating even asbestos, a substance with devastating health impacts that are beyond argument.

The CSIA has language in Section 6 saying that the safety determination for existing chemicals should be made based on risk, but because of the way it is drafted the cost-benefit considerations are not fully separated and the "least burdensome" requirement is effectively retained for bans and phaseouts. While the intent of the bill may be to require a risk-only determination in this section, that intent is not realized. In fact, our reading of the legislation is that EPA would still not be able to ban asbestos under the section as drafted.

But there is the additional problem that the "unreasonable risk" standard is also invoked in Sections 4 and 5 where there is no qualifying language suggesting a new meaning. In Section 4, EPA is directed to identify chemicals as "low priority" based on a determination that they are "likely to meet the safety standard." Those chemicals are set aside for no further action or scrutiny. In Section 5, the EPA is directed to apply the same test to a new chemical before it is allowed on the market. This is one of the bill's major selling points—that it imposes a safety screen of some kind on new chemicals for the first time. However, since "unreasonable risk" has such a clear meaning in the legislative history and case law of TSCA, it would almost certainly have the same old meaning, and therefore the same old problems, in these sections.

The simplest way to avoid these problems is choosing a different standard that signals a clear break with TSCA, such as "reasonable certainty of no harm" which is currently used in the pesticide program. If the legislation continues to use "unreasonable risk" it should be clearly redefined in the definitions section of the bill to be explicitly health only. That clear break would end the ambiguity anywhere the term is used in the bill and reduce the risk of litigation. Section 6 should also be redrafted to truly end the "least burdensome" requirement and simplify the cost-benefit considerations for risk management measures.

Safety Determinations

Recent National Academy of Sciences reports, the American Academy of Pediatrics, and the broad public health and environmental community agree that safety determinations should protect vulnerable populations and account for the aggregate exposure to a chemical. Though grounded in science, both concepts also make common sense and are relatively easy to understand. They were at the core of the bipartisan reform of pesticide law, the Food Quality Protection Act (FQPA) of 1996. Neither concept is adequately reflected in the CSIA, though they are mentioned in ways that suggest some intent to incorporate them.

Vulnerable populations refers to the fact that a given chemical will affect me—as a relatively healthy 200 lb. adult male in Washington, DC—differently than it affects a child, a pregnant woman, or someone who lives or works in a heavily contaminated environment. Many chemicals, particularly those that mimic hormones, have substantially more impact on the developing fetus or child than on an adult. The vast body of peer-reviewed science on this subject over the last twenty years has helped put chemical reform on the national agenda. A 1993 National Academy of Sciences study, "Pesticides in the Diets of Infants and Children," found that a failure to account for vulnerable populations meant that EPA decisions about pesticides did not protect children from exposure to the pesticide residues on food. Congress responded with the FQPA in 1996 to ensure that they did. It would be odd for Congress, after all these years, to reform our chemical policies in ways that did not provide a similar assurance for chemicals. Vulnerable populations should be defined in the legislation. Safety assessments should be required to identify them for a given chemical, and any risk management measure should be required to protect them.

Aggregate exposure is a fancy term for the basic fact that we are often exposed to the same chemical from multiple sources. That means that the dose of the chemical that we receive is bigger than the dose from any one exposure, in the same way that taking three pills of a prescription drug represents a bigger dose than one pill. A pregnant woman, for example, might be exposed to the same chemical from multiple consumer products in her home, a process at her workplace, and—if the chemical is also a pollutant—from the air or water. If safety assessments don't take the aggregate exposure into account, they will simply be wrong. They will not reflect what is happening in the real world and the resulting risk management measures won't make a difference in the real world. The legislation should require EPA to assess the aggregate exposure to a chemical unless it determines that any vulnerable populations it identifies are not exposed to the chemical from more than one source.

Our coalition prefers the "reasonable certainty of no harm" standard in part because it incorporates these concepts automatically given its history in the pesticide law. If Congress retains the "unreasonable risk" standard in the legislation, the safety determinations must include vulnerable populations and aggregate exposure as core concepts. (This also could be done in a new definition of "unreasonable risk.") Otherwise, Congress will not be able to claim that the legislation protects pregnant women and children and heavily contaminated communities from chemicals as they are actually used.

Testing and Information Requirements

The CSIA allows EPA to require testing on an existing chemical by order rather than by the more cumbersome rulemaking process. That is a significant improvement for which its authors deserve credit. At the same time, this improvement is constrained by the fact that EPA can require testing only for existing chemicals under the bill if it has designated them as high priority. That creates a few problems.

First, it means that EPA can only prioritize chemicals based on existing information, rather than any new testing data. The information available for most chemicals is relatively limited (a legacy of TSCA's overly burdensome process for testing.) That, in turn, means that a chemical could be designated as low priority based on inadequate information. Under the bill, these chemicals are then effectively set aside forever at both the federal and state level, unless new information becomes available. It is unclear where that information would come from. Industry would have no incentive to develop it, and EPA would not be allowed to order it under the bill. In addition, if EPA has to put anything that it thinks needs some testing in the high-priority category it will certainly slow down that process. An obvious solution is to allow EPA to order testing for purposes of prioritization, not just for purposes of a safety determination, and to require adequate information for a low-priority designation.

In addition, the CSIA requires EPA to tier testing requirements in an overly rigid way. A chemical would have to raise a red flag from a screening-level test before EPA can order a more extensive test. There are not effective screening-level tests that predict some of the health end points about which the public is most concerned. Where these end points are a concern, the EPA should be able to move straight to the more

Overview of the Toxic Substances Control Act

The Toxic Substances Control Act [TSCA] granted EPA [Environmental Protection Agency] authority to create a regulatory framework to collect data on chemicals in order to evaluate, assess, mitigate, and control risks that may be posed by their manufacture, processing, and use. TSCA provides a variety of control methods to prevent chemicals from posing unreasonable risk.

TSCA standards may apply at any point during a chemical's life cycle. Under TSCA Section 5, EPA has established an inventory of chemical substances. If a chemical is not already on the inventory, and has not been excluded by TSCA, a premanufacture notice (PMN) must be submitted to EPA before manufacture or import. The PMN must identify the chemical and provide available information on health and environmental effects. If available data are not sufficient to evaluate the chemical's effects, EPA can impose restrictions pending the development of information on its health and environmental effects. EPA can also restrict significant new uses of chemicals based on factors such as the projected volume and use of the chemical.

Under TSCA Section 6, EPA can ban manufacture or distribution in commerce, limit use, require labeling, or place other restrictions on chemicals that pose unreasonable risks. Among the chemicals EPA regulates under Section 6 authority are asbestos, chlorofluorocarbons (CFCs), lead, and polychlorinated biphenyls (PCBs).

"Toxic Substances Control Act (TSCA),"
EPA.gov, 2014.

relevant test. The tiered testing requirements in the bill should be eased to ensure that needed tests aren't prevented.

Finally, the CSIA takes away EPA's ability to require testing for new chemicals. The way it is drafted suggests that change may have been inadvertent, but this authority should be restored.

Confidential Business Information

The public interest community and most of regulated industry have agreed for some time that TSCA's provisions for CBI are too often abused. In addition, the burgeoning "secret inventory" of chemicals undermines the transparency of the program. The absurd consequence is that you can see there is a chemical on the inventory that causes cancer, you just can't find out which chemical.

The CSIA creates new rules of the road for justifying CBI claims that are an improvement, but it strangely grandfathers in existing claims, including those whose abuses fueled calls for reform. The grandfathering should be removed. In addition, the CSIA enshrines the concept of a secret inventory in the law for the first time. Further debate and discussion are needed to find a solution on the issue of chemical identity that does not threaten public health and the environment.

"Frameworks" and Science Guidance

There are six subsections in Section 4 and two in Section 6 of the CSIA that require the EPA to develop new "frameworks," policies and guidance on both procedures for the program and scientific questions like evaluating the reliability of data. These policies are also subject to notice and comment and judicial review. Simply completing these frameworks on the most optimistic schedule would take several years. If EPA is prevented from getting started evaluating chemicals until these policies are in place, it will lead to substantial delay in the entire program.

In addition, this section of the bill uses various terms of art in ways that are mostly undefined and which will encourage litigation over the ambiguities. In at least one instance, the bill takes a stand on a particular science question that contradicts the National Academy of Sciences recommendations.

These sections of the legislation could simply be eliminated. The EPA already has guidance and polices on most of the questions—like prioritization and assessment methodologies. At the very least these sections should be consolidated with careful attention to avoiding new handles for litigation or unacceptably delaying the start of the new program. If science guidance is needed, it should reflect, rather than contradict, the recommendations of the National Academy of Sciences.

State Preemption

One of TSCA's only clear successes is that it allowed states to develop their own chemical policies and restrictions unless they conflict with a federal regulation. Even then, it allowed states to seek a waiver for their own restrictions or to ban a chemical outright. Since the TSCA program never really got off the ground, states have played the leading role in regulating chemicals over the last 36 years. Many states have banned particular chemicals of concern—like mercury, cadmium and bisphenol A—from particular categories of products. A handful—California, Maine, Washington, and Minnesota—have developed more comprehensive policies that address broader classes of chemicals. These policies have improved public health and environmental quality.

CSIA would preempt state restrictions on a chemical at the point at which EPA prioritizes the chemical as either high or low. Low-priority chemicals are those that EPA is setting aside based on a review that is, by definition, short of a full safety determination. This more cursory review does not justify that level of protection for a chemical. For high priority chemicals, on the other hand, it could be years between the prioritization of the chemical and the decision that it is either safe, or that it is unsafe and requires risk management measures. In the meantime, states would be prevented from taking action on what are, by definition, the riskier chemicals. The proposed new waiver process for states is overly cumbersome compared to the existing one. The states' ability to co-enforce federal requirements is removed. Finally, while an attempt has been made in the bill to preserve state warning and information requirements, which have been some of the most effective, the language ultimately does not protect them.

The more protective approach to states' rights in the current TSCA largely worked as intended. States were allowed to move forward even as the federal program became bogged down in ways that surely none of its authors intended. Congress should apply that lesson to the CSIA.

Deadlines, Minimum Requirements, and Funding

One of the lessons of TSCA is that it lacked deadlines or goals for how many existing chemicals should be reviewed or how long assessments should take. The new chemicals program, on the other hand, had clear deadlines for how quickly EPA had to respond to a premanufacture notice. As a result, most of the activity at EPA under TSCA has been in the new chemicals program. Also, other laws administered by the EPA generally had deadlines for listing pollutants or making decisions, pushing TSCA's existing chemicals program to the back of the line in a bureaucratic environment of limited resources.

The CSIA repeats this mistake. It should be amended to add deadlines for critical policy decisions and for the minimum number of chemicals assessed, either per year, or over some longer time frame. Reform should also contain a new source of dedicated funding for the program, such as a user fee. Appropriate deadlines and work requirements would drive action at the agency and help both Congress and the public to hold the agency accountable.

The Low-Priority Category

Finally, we would urge the committee to consider whether the legislation should have a low-priority category at all. The goal of reform should be to protect public health and the environment from the risks posed by chemicals. Public confidence will follow if that goal is being met and benefits to the business community will follow on top of that. A modest but credible program will still produce tangible results.

The low-priority category in the bill adds a level of murkiness to the program that will likely undermine its credibility. For high-priority chemicals—if all the appropriate fixes are made—the public will know that a chemical is either safe or that its risks are being adequately controlled. Low-priority chemicals, however, are effectively being treated as safe even though they haven't really been found to be safe. Furthermore, EPA resources will be diverted into deciding what goes into this murky category rather than focused where they should be: taking action on the riskiest chemicals.

Earlier, I proposed changes that limit the damage from this category—requiring adequate information, breaking the link to preemption, clarifying the standard, etc. But with limited resources likely to be the norm for the foreseeable future, Congress should consider focusing those resources on a single category of priority chemicals.

A Broader Reform

This is not an exhaustive list of either the problems with the CSIA or its positive attributes, but it does provide the committee with the areas of the bill that we believe require the most attention. In general, the bill needs a substantial reworking and rebalancing in favor of delivering clearer health and environmental benefits sooner and reducing the risks of paralysis and delay. There are provisions from previous reform proposals, such as expedited action on persistent, bioaccumulative and toxic (PBT) chemicals and "hot spot" communities that would help effect such a rebalancing if incorporated. I've focused my testimony instead on the core areas within the framework of the CSIA and where we see them falling short of the critical elements needed for reform to be meaningful and credible. We hope Congress will consider these recommendations and craft legislation that provides the public with the appropriate oversight of chemicals that is long overdue.

> "BPA has become common. It is used widely to harden plastics and as a coating inside cans of beverages and food."

Bisphenol A (BPA) Should Be Banned

Karl Grossman

Karl Grossman is an author, a professor of journalism at the State University of New York/College at Old Westbury, and an associate at Fairness and Accuracy in Reporting (FAIR). In the following viewpoint, he reports on a 2012 law passed by the Suffolk County legislature in New York banning receipts coated with the chemical bisphenol A (BPA), which has been found to carry a risk of breast and prostate cancer, obesity, diabetes, developmental problems, infertility, and a range of other health issues. Studies reveal that workers who frequently handle BPA-coated receipts have higher levels of BPA in their systems. The law penalizes businesses found to use BPA-coated receipts and forces a transition to safer alternatives. Grossman argues that this law is a welcome step in the fight for public health and urges local governments to extend BPA bans to the use of all plastics and other products that contain BPA.

As you read, consider the following questions:

1. According to Grossman, in what year did the Suffolk County legislature enact a first-in-the-nation law to prohibit the use of bisphenol A (BPA) in baby bottles and sippy cups?

2. How much more BPA does the average employee who works in a job where BPA-coated thermal paper is frequently used have in their bodies than workers in other professions?

3. What are the penalties for the first violation of the Stern law, according to the author?

It's what the county legislature in Suffolk County, New York, is noted for—passing first-in-the-nation laws. It's done that with laws banning the handheld use of cell phones while driving, the sale of drop-side cribs and the supplement ephedra, and many statutes prohibiting smoking in public places. The measures have often been replicated statewide and nationally.

And the panel did it again this month [December 2012] passing a measure that bans receipts coated with the chemical BPA. BPA, the acronym for bisphenol A, has been found to be a cause of cancer and other health maladies.

"Once again this institution is going to set the standard for other states to follow," declared legislator Steve Stern of Huntington after the passage of his bill December 4.

The top elected official of Suffolk County, which encompasses eastern Long Island, County Executive Steve Bellone plans to sign the measure into law next week.

The Dangers of BPA

BPA has become common. It is used widely to harden plastics and as a coating inside cans of beverages and food. Another use is coating the paper used for receipts enabling it to become "thermal paper" and react to heat to print numbers and words.

In 2009, the Suffolk County legislature enacted a first-in-the-nation law—also authored by Stern—prohibiting the use of BPA in baby bottles and other beverage containers used by children under three. Stern was made aware of the health dangers of BPA by Karen Joy Miller, founder of Prevention Is the Cure, an initiative of the Huntington Breast Cancer Action Coalition. Prevention Is the Cure emphasizes the elimination of the causes of cancer.

Ms. Miller testified at the legislative session at which the measure passed 16 to 1: "We've got to end this disease [cancer], and a bad-acting chemical like [BPA] is at the top of the list." After the vote, she applauded "Legislator Stern and the Suffolk County legislature for taking this important step to protect public health."

Stern's "Safer Sales Slip Act" was also backed by Dr. Philip Landrigan, chair of the Department of Preventive Medicine and dean for Global Health with the Children's Environmental Health Center at Mount Sinai [Hospital] in New York City. It will protect "the health of the public by reducing exposures to BPA for all Suffolk County families and, most especially, pregnant or nursing women, and women of childbearing age.... As leaders in pediatrics and preventive medicine, we strongly support this legislation."

Meanwhile, claiming at the legislative session that BPA is safe was Stephen Rosario of the American Chemistry Council. Millions of tons of BPA are now manufactured annually and the American Chemistry Council has led in defending the substance.

The Stern Bill

The Stern bill declares that the Suffolk legislature "finds and determines that BPA is a synthetic estrogen which disrupts healthy development and can lead to an altered immune sys-

Products Where BPA Is Found

BPA [bisphenol A] is used to make polycarbonate plastics that are commonly used in consumer products such as baby bottles, sippy cups, and reusable water bottles. BPA is often found in epoxy resins used to coat metal food and beverage cans, including beer and soda cans. BPA is also used in the production of other plastics, including those used for medical devices, for industrial applications (such as adhesives and paints), and in the production of flame retardants and thermal paper (such as those used in cash register receipts). Some polymers used in dental sealants and tooth coatings also contain BPA.

"Congress Must Protect Children
from a Developmental Toxic: Bisphenol A (BPA),"
Natural Resources Defense Council, July 2010.

tem, hyperactivity, learning disabilities, reproductive health problems, increased risk of breast and prostate cancer, obesity and diabetes."

It refers to his earlier "Toxin-Free Toddlers and Babies Act" and notes that since the passage of "this groundbreaking ban," a national counterpart of the measure was enacted— "finally, this summer"—by the U.S. Food and Drug Administration.

Of receipts coated with BPA, the BPA on this "thermal paper can transfer onto anything it contacts, including skin" and through the skin "be absorbed . . . into the body," says the bill.

This "dermal exposure to BPA poses a risk to public health and particularly to those whose employment requires distribution of such receipts." Moreover, "the thermal paper containing BPA is also utilized in bank receipts and at automated teller machines and gas pump receipts, creating multiple and ubiquitous points of exposure in daily life."

Further, research has determined that "workers employed at retail and food service industries, where BPA-containing thermal paper is most commonly used, have an average of 30% more BPA in their bodies than adults employed in other professions."

And, critically, as the measure notes, "there are several manufacturers that produce thermal paper that does not contain BPA." That's the way it is for toxic products and processes: There are safe alternatives for them. There are safe substitutes for virtually every deadly product and process. The problem: the vested interests that continue to push and defend them.

The Stern law carries penalties of $500 for the first violation and $1,000 "for each subsequent violation."

It hopefully will be replicated far and wide. And, bans on BPA should be extended to the use of all plastics with BPA, along with cans of beverages and food that have a coating of this poison inside.

> *"Politically driven substitutes will always be second to the products that won in the marketplace. Thus, unless there is a verified and significant risk, banning products isn't a good idea."*

Bisphenol A (BPA) Should Not Be Banned

Angela Logomasini

Angela Logomasini is a senior fellow at the Competitive Enterprise Institute. In the following viewpoint, she asserts that banning bisphenol A (BPA) is unnecessary and could even imperil public health. A number of scientific panels around the world have investigated BPA only to find that it does not pose a public health risk. In the United States, numerous studies by the Food and Drug Administration (FDA) have failed to find any actionable evidence that BPA endangers public health. Yet activist petitions, lobbying, and media campaigns have prompted health authorities to launch more investigations and an industry-driven ban on BPA in baby bottles and sippy cups. Logomasini predicts that this ban will lead to more calls for a total ban, which would be a mistake. BPA resins are effective in controlling foodborne pathogens, and some authorities worry that a BPA ban would result in an increase in serious foodborne illnesses.

As you read, consider the following questions:

1. According to the author, what countries have investigated the use of bisphenol A (BPA) and found no significant health risk?

2. Who requested the ban on BPA in baby bottles and sippy cups, according to Logomasini?

3. What kind of dangerous foodborne pathogens does the author maintain BPA resins control?

This past July [2012] the Food and Drug Administration (FDA) banned the use of the chemical bisphenol A (BPA) to make baby bottles and sippy cups. Environmental activists would like you to believe the move was designed to protect public health and that more bans are necessary. But the greens are wrong on both counts—and their advice could imperil public health.

For more than 50 years, manufacturers have safely used BPA to make hard, clear plastics for food containers, medical devices, safety goggles, and more. They also make resins that line aluminum and steel cans to reduce contamination of food and extend shelf life.

BPA's Alleged Risks

Much of BPA's alleged risk to humans is based on studies of rodents that were administered massive doses, often by injection. The relevance of these studies to humans who are exposed to trace amounts in food is highly questionable. In addition, activists have attempted to use a number of studies conducted on humans to make their case even though reputable scientific bodies around the world have dismissed these studies as seriously flawed or inconclusive.

Activists also condemn BPA simply because it shows up in human urine. All this fact proves is that the human body, unlike rodents, quickly metabolizes BPA without ill effects. An

EPA [Environmental Protection Agency]-funded study conducted on human volunteers who were exposed to high levels of BPA underscored this point. The chemical passed through the humans quickly, never reaching levels that pose problems to rodents.

Scientific panels around the world have investigated BPA many times—examining the full body of research and focusing on the best science available. In Japan, the European Union, Canada, Norway, France and elsewhere, researchers have found no public health risk related to consumer exposure to BPA. Even the Environmental Protection Agency—which is well known for exaggerating chemical risks—states that consumer exposure to BPA is likely 100 to 1,000 times lower than EPA's estimated safe-exposure levels for both infants and adults.

Because of activist group petitions, lobbying, and media campaigns, the FDA has continued to spend taxpayer dollars to study and restudy BPA during the past several years, but it has not been able to find a serious risk. Even as the agency issued its ban on BPA bottles and sippy cups, a representative explained to the *New York Times*: "based on all the evidence, we continue to support its [BPA's] safe use."

The ban came at the request of industry rather than to address health problems. The American Chemistry Council (ACC) explained in a press statement: "Although governments around the world continue to support the safety of BPA in food contact materials, confusion about whether BPA is used in baby bottles and sippy cups had become an unnecessary distraction to consumers, legislators and state regulators." Accordingly, the ACC supported a ban because it "provides certainty that BPA is not used to make the baby bottles and sippy cups on store shelves, either today or in the future."

But green groups use this industry-driven ban to advance a larger anti-BPA crusade. "This is only a baby step in the fight to eradicate BPA," says Sarah Janssen of the Natural Resources Defense Council in a press release. "To truly protect the public, FDA needs to ban BPA from all food packaging," she explains.

Janssen offers seriously bad advice because BPA resins control dangerous foodborne pathogens such as *E. coli* and botulism. And there are no good alternative products to replace BPA resins.

In fact, packaging manufacturers have responded to the politically charged debate on BPA during the past several years by attempting to find alternatives—without much success. One industry representative told the *Washington Post*, "We don't have a safe, effective alternative, and that's an unhappy place to be. . . . No one wants to talk about that." As a result, BPA resin bans may eventually translate into an increase in serious foodborne illnesses.

BPA Is Safe

Still, some people argue that we should at least seek substitutes to "be on the safe side." They forget that every product of the market prevailed because it was the best to perform the job at an acceptable price at the time. Politically driven substitutes will always be second to the products that won in the marketplace. Thus, unless there is a verified and significant risk, banning products isn't a good idea.

Banning safe, useful products simply wastes investment that went into designing them, discourages innovators who fear similar repercussions, and diverts resources from useful enterprises into production of second-best substitutes. And for consumers, the result can be dangerous.

"For the average American, it's tempting to want to dismiss the danger: surely chemical plants are located far away from where you live, right?"

Regulations on Chemical Production and Storage Should Be Tightened

John Deans and Richard Moore

Richard Moore is the coordinator of the Los Jardines Institute, and John Deans is a toxics campaigner at Greenpeace. In the following viewpoint, they assess the danger of chemical production and storage on the American public, noting that one in three Americans lives close enough to a chemical facility to be at risk of death or illness due to chemical exposure. The transport of chemicals compounds the danger for average Americans. Moore and Deans maintain that the prevalence of risk means that it is time to impose more stringent regulations on the chemicals industry, especially when it comes to shipping and stockpiling deadly toxins. They find overwhelming public support for such regulation and report on a growing number of Americans who

John Deans and Richard Moore, "Will the EPA Force Chemical Plants to Go Safe?" Reprinted with permission from the August 13, 2012 issue of *The Nation*. For subscription information, call 1-800-333-8536. Portions of each week's *Nation* magazine can be accessed at http://www.thenation.com.

are urging the Environmental Protection Agency to create new regulations to protect the American public from dangerous chemical exposure.

As you read, consider the following questions:

1. According to the authors, how many chemical facilities in the United States each put more than one hundred thousand people at risk of death or illness due to chemical exposure?

2. According to a recent poll, what percentage of the American people believe that the United States needs better regulation of toxic chemicals?

3. How many people do the authors report recently signed a petition calling for safer chemical plants?

On August 7 [2012], the Chevron refinery in Richmond, California, had a serious fire that forced local residents to hide in their homes with the doors and windows sealed, and sent hundreds seeking medical care. If the explosion had ruptured one of the tanks of anhydrous ammonia on site, 160,000 residents living up to five miles from the plant may have found themselves in a blanket of poison gas.

A Real Danger for Average Americans

For the average American, it's tempting to want to dismiss the danger: surely chemical plants are located far away from where you live, right?

Likely, you're wrong. A shocking number of chemical plants are located in or near the hearts of major US urban areas. In the Greater Los Angeles area, KIK SoCal's facility puts almost five million people at risk. Nearly 4 million Dallas residents live in the shadow of the Dallas Central Regional Wastewater System. In the Northeast, the Kuehne plant near Manhattan endangers more than 12 million people.

These are only a few examples—nationwide, there are almost 500 chemical facilities that each put more than 100,000 people at risk of death or illness due to chemical exposure. These plants use toxic chemicals like chlorine, phosgene, hydrofluoric acid and other dangerous substances that, when accidents occur, cause catastrophic loss of life.

In fact, one in three people in this country live in the danger zones around the highest risk plants. Even people who don't live next door to a chemical facility are still in harm's way: chemicals are shipped around the country by truck and train, meaning that it's likely that the vast majority of us encounter this threat at some time or another. A horrifying example is the train derailment in Graniteville, South Carolina, on January 9, 2005, that killed nine people and exposed at least 250 to chlorine gas, costing tens of millions of dollars. It's time we stop chemical companies from shipping and stockpiling deadly toxins.

Passing Legislation on Safer Chemical Facilities

Congress may be nearly incapable of accomplishing anything, but fortunately for us, the Environmental Protection Agency [EPA] has the authority to use the Clean Air Act to require safeguards at our nation's chemical plants. The EPA never fully implemented the "Bhopal Amendment" of 1990, which requires chemical facilities to prevent a release of ultrahazardous substances. President [Barack] Obama has consistently called for legislation that would prioritize the use of safer chemical processes to prevent disasters at the most dangerous chemical facilities.

The president has nearly the entire nation behind him on this. When polled, over 70 percent of the population thinks we need better regulation of toxic chemicals. National security experts have said for at least a decade that these "prepositioned weapons of mass destruction" are a weak link in

The Bhopal Disaster

Industrial accidents include events involving harm or death of a single on-site employee to catastrophes that kill, harm, or displace hundreds of thousands of people. The largest industrial accident in history occurred in Bhopal, India, in December 1984. A chemical leak from a Union Carbide pesticide plant in the city sent a toxic cloud of methyl isocyanate and other chemicals through the city. Over 3,000 people died in the immediate aftermath of the industrial accident and approximately 15,000 to 20,000 people died subsequently. An additional 50,000 people suffered permanent disabilities, including blindness.

The Bhopal disaster also demonstrates how a single, catastrophic industrial disaster can have long-term health and environmental consequences. Despite government claims to the contrary, recent studies show that the Bhopal disaster contaminated the area's groundwater. Two independent water surveys conducted in 2009 found unsafe levels of several toxic chemicals and heavy metals in Bhopal's drinking water—some at 1,000 times the World Health Organization's recommended level. Bhopal continues to suffer a birth defect rate ten times that of other communities in India of similar socioeconomic status.

"Industrial Accidents and Pollution,"
Global Issues in Context Online Collection, 2014.

our critical infrastructure. Workers in dangerous facilities want a safer place to work. Communities on train and truck routes to and from these facilities want to be safe, as do communities near the plants themselves. Health experts and first responders know they couldn't handle the massive casualties caused by a disaster. Railroad companies have said they no longer want to ship these poison gases.

In fact, the only entities standing in the way are the chemical companies, their armies of lobbyists and the politicians they've bought off. But even in the industry, some companies like Clorox are doing the right thing, eliminating the disaster risk from their facilities by converting to safer—affordable— chemical processes that eliminate the need to store large amounts of poison gases. For example, instead of using the chemical weapon, chlorine gas, to make bleach, some makers have switched to using electrolysis to turn salt into the chlorine as needed. Still, the chemical industry is fighting to preserve the status quo.

A Plan of Action

That's why a coalition of over 100 organizations representing workers, environmental justice leaders and health professionals sent the president a letter over a year ago asking him to take action. More recently, over 60,000 people signed a petition calling for safer chemical plants and fifty-nine organizations filed an official petition with the EPA. Under the 1990 "Bhopal Amendment" to the Clean Air Act, facilities that store and use highly toxic substances are required to prevent releases of those chemicals through safe operation. The EPA has authority to both provide new guidance and create new regulations, but the policy has never been fully implemented. Preventing disasters by using safer chemical processes should be the cornerstone of this program. Governor Christine Todd Whitman was head of the EPA in 2002 when they tried to implement such a program and she has recently recommended this action to current administrator Lisa Jackson.

Every day that goes by is one too many for the people living this dangerous game of disaster roulette. Politicians have delayed a decision on chemical security for a decade. It is time for President Obama to authorize the EPA to fully implement chemical disaster prevention under the Clean Air Act.

Periodical and Internet Sources Bibliography

The following articles have been selected to supplement the diverse views presented in this chapter.

Cal Dooley	"Update Chemical Regulation: Another View," *USA Today*, February 17, 2014.
Jen Landa	"The Dangers of BPA," *Huffington Post*, March 7, 2014.
Jason Plautz	"Why Congress Can't Fix Our Crazy Chemical Safety System," *National Journal*, May 1, 2014.
Brad Plumer	"After 37 Years, U.S. Chemical-Safety Laws May Finally Get an Overhaul," *Washington Post*, May 22, 2013.
Stewart M. Powell and Charles J. Lewis	"Regulation of Chemical Industry Haphazard, Toothless," *Houston Chronicle*, April 27, 2013.
Erica Salcuni	"Infants and Unborn Babies Harmed by BPA Chemicals in Plastic," *Guardian Liberty Voice* (Las Vegas, NV), April 30, 2014.
Kate Sheppard	"These Companies Want More Government Regulation," *Huffington Post*, December 11, 2013.
Bryan Walsh	"Why the FDA Hasn't Banned Potentially Toxic BPA (Yet)," *Time*, April 3, 2012.
Amy Westervelt	"A Threat and a Promise: Changing US Policies on Toxic Chemicals," *Guardian*, March 28, 2014.
Christine Todd Whitman	"Whitman: How to Improve Chemical Plant Safety," *USA Today*, February 20, 2014.
Amanda Woerner	"BPA Linked to Higher Risk for Obesity Among Young Girls," Fox News, June 13, 2013.

For Further Discussion

Chapter 1

1. Julie Gunlock argues that alarmists often strike fear into parents by warning them of the everyday dangers their children face due to chemical exposure. She believes that parents should ignore many of these warnings. Do you agree with Gunlock? Why, or why not?

2. According to James Hamblin, children from low-income families are most susceptible to the dangers of toxic chemical exposure. What reasons does Hamblin give for making this claim? After reading the viewpoint, do you agree with Hamblin's argument? Explain your reasoning.

Chapter 2

1. Sally Satel argues that e-cigarettes could benefit the American public by helping millions of people stop smoking, thus reducing the amount of chemicals smokers subject themselves and others to. What recommendations does Satel provide to encourage the use of e-cigarettes among adult smokers? Do you think these suggestions will be effective? Why, or why not? Can you think of additional recommendations to promote the use of e-cigarettes over traditional cigarettes? Explain.

2. Linda Sharps asserts that many cosmetics contain harmful chemicals. In your opinion, should people limit their use of cosmetics? Explain your answer.

Chapter 3

1. James Salzman discusses the safety of drinking water and the dangers posed to the nation's water supply. Discuss some of the threats mentioned by Salzman. What does Salzman recommend to protect the water supply? Do you think these tactics will be effective? Explain.

2. Sandy Dechert argues that hydraulic fracturing negatively affects the environment and could cause health problems. Nicolas D. Loris contends that hydraulic fracturing is a vital part of the United States' energy production and economic growth. After reading both viewpoints, do you believe the benefits of hydraulic fracturing outweigh the risks? Explain.

3. David Westerholm examines the effectiveness of using dispersants after an oil spill. What is Westerholm's stance on the issue? Based on his argument, do you think using dispersants in the Deepwater Horizon disaster was justifiable? Explain.

Chapter 4

1. According to Jon Entine, banning certain chemicals would be more harmful than beneficial. Do you agree or disagree with Entine? Explain your reasoning.

2. Karl Grossman asserts that bisphenol A (BPA) is dangerous and should be banned. Conversely, Angela Logomasini contends that BPA does not pose a significant health risk and should not be banned. With which author do you agree, and why?

3. John Deans and Richard Moore argue that the production and storage of chemicals are extremely dangerous and put many people at risk of illness or death due to chemical exposure. Do you think that their call for tighter regulations on toxic chemicals will help protect Americans who live near chemical facilities? Explain. Cite some other tactics that could be used to prevent chemical exposure.

Organizations to Contact

The editors have compiled the following list of organizations concerned with the issues debated in this book. The descriptions are derived from materials provided by the organizations. All have publications or information available for interested readers. The list was compiled on the date of publication of the present volume; the information provided here may change. Be aware that many organizations take several weeks or longer to respond to inquiries, so allow as much time as possible.

American Council on Science and Health (ACSH)

1995 Broadway, Suite 202, New York, NY   10023-5882
(212) 362-7044 • fax: (212) 362-4919
e-mail: acsh@acsh.org
website: www.acsh.org

The American Council on Science and Health (ACSH) is a consumer education consortium concerned with environmental and health-related issues. The council publishes the daily *Dispatch* and articles such as "Natural Foods Have No Chemicals—Right? Think Again" and "Some Common Sense on Agricultural Pesticides from a Genuine Expert," which are available on its website.

CropLife America

1156 Fifteenth Street NW, Washington, DC   20005
(202) 296-1585 • fax: (202) 463-0474
website: www.croplifeamerica.org

CropLife America is an association of firms that produce agricultural chemicals such as herbicides, pesticides, defoliants, and soil disinfectants. It contains legislative and regulatory departments and maintains committees on environmental management, public health, and toxicology. The organization promotes the use of chemicals in farm production. Its website includes a section titled "For Researchers & Students," which contains an array of resources on crop protection, pesticides, and related topics.

Earthjustice

50 California Street, Suite 500, San Francisco, CA   94111
(800) 584-6460
e-mail: info@earthjustice.org
website: earthjustice.org

Earthjustice is a nonprofit environmental law organization that fights to protect human health, preserve the wild, advance clean energy, and combat climate change. The organization's group of attorneys works to uphold environmental laws. Its website offers articles such as "Targeting the Most Dangerous Chemicals" as well as information on cases in litigation.

Environmental Defense Fund (EDF)

257 Park Avenue South, New York, NY   10010
(800) 684-3322
website: www.edf.org

Founded by scientists in 1967, the Environmental Defense Fund (EDF) conducts original research and enlists outside experts to solve environmental problems. The advocacy group forms partnerships with corporations to promote environmentally friendly business practices. On its website, EDF offers news, fact sheets, articles, and reports such as *Toxics Across America.*

Environmental Protection Agency (EPA)

1200 Pennsylvania Avenue NW, Washington, DC   20460
(202) 272-0167
website: www.epa.gov

The Environmental Protection Agency (EPA) is the federal agency in charge of protecting human health and the environment. The agency works toward these goals by enacting and enforcing regulations, assisting businesses and local environmental agencies, and identifying and solving environmental problems. The EPA publishes speeches, testimony, periodic reports, and regional news on its website.

Food and Drug Administration (FDA)
10903 New Hampshire Avenue, Silver Spring, MD 20993
(888) 463-6332
website: www.fda.gov

The Food and Drug Administration (FDA) is a federal government public health agency that monitors the safety of the nation's foods and medicines. Its website includes a special section that focuses on foodborne illness and contaminants. Among its publications is *Bad Bug Book: Handbook of Foodborne Pathogenic Microorganisms and Natural Toxins.*

Friends of the Earth
1100 Fifteenth Street NW, 11th Floor, Washington, DC 20005
(877) 843-8687 • fax: (202) 783-0444
e-mail: foe@foe.org
website: www.foe.org

Friends of the Earth is a national advocacy organization dedicated to protecting the planet from environmental degradation; preserving biological, cultural, and ethnic diversity; and empowering citizens to have an influential voice in decisions affecting the quality of their environment. It publishes the quarterly *Friends of the Earth Newsmagazine*, recent and archived issues of which are available on its website along with fact sheets, news, articles, and reports.

Natural Resources Defense Council (NRDC)
40 West Twentieth Street, New York, NY 10011
(212) 727-2700 • fax: (212) 727-1773
e-mail: nrdcinfo@nrdc.org
website: www.nrdc.org

The Natural Resources Defense Council (NRDC) is a nonprofit organization that uses both law and science to protect the planet's wildlife and wild places and to ensure a safe and healthy environment for all living things. NRDC publishes the magazine *OnEarth* and the bulletin *Nature's Voice*. On its website, NRDC provides links to specific environmental topics as well as news, articles, and reports.

Sierra Club

85 Second Street, 2nd Floor, San Francisco, CA 94105
(415) 977-5500 • fax: (415) 977-5797
e-mail: information@sierraclub.org
website: www.sierraclub.org

The Sierra Club is an environmental organization working to protect and restore the natural and human environment. Among the organization's goals are controlling pollution and minimizing waste residuals with special care of hazardous materials. The Sierra Club publishes the magazine *Sierra* and the e-newsletter *Sierra Club Insider.*

Union of Concerned Scientists (UCS)

2 Brattle Square, Cambridge, MA 02138-3780
(617) 547-5552 • fax: (617) 864-9405
website: www.ucsusa.org

The Union of Concerned Scientists (UCS) aims to advance responsible public policy in areas where science and technology play important roles. Its programs emphasize transportation reform, arms control, safe and renewable energy technologies, and sustainable agriculture. UCS publications include the magazine *Catalyst* and the quarterly newsletter *Earthwise.*

World Health Organization (WHO)

Avenue Appia 20, Geneva 27 1211
   Switzerland
+ 41 22 791 21 11 • fax: + 41 22 791 31 11
website: www.who.int/en

The World Health Organization (WHO) is the authority for health within the United Nations system. The organization's responsibilities include providing leadership on global health matters, setting norms and standards, and assessing health trends. Many publications can be found on WHO's website, including *Guidelines on the Prevention of Toxic Exposures.*

Worldwatch Institute
1400 Sixteenth Street NW, Suite 430, Washington, DC   20036
(202) 745-8092
e-mail: worldwatch@worldwatch.org
website: www.worldwatch.org

Worldwatch Institute is a nonprofit public policy research organization dedicated to informing the public and policy makers about emerging global problems and trends and the complex links between the environment and the world economy. Its publications include *Vital Signs*, issued annually; the bimonthly magazine *World Watch*; and numerous policy papers.

Bibliography of Books

Diana S. Aga, ed.   *Fate of Pharmaceuticals in the Environment and in Water Treatment Systems.* Boca Raton, FL: CRC Press, 2012.

Dan Agin   *More than Genes: What Science Can Tell Us About Toxic Chemicals, Development, and the Risk to Our Children.* New York: Oxford University Press, 2010.

Nena Baker   *The Body Toxic: How the Hazardous Chemistry of Everyday Things Threatens Our Health and Well-Being.* New York: North Point Press, 2008.

David O. Carpenter, ed.   *Effects of Persistent and Bioactive Organic Pollutants on Human Health.* Hoboken, NJ: John Wiley & Sons, 2013.

Debra Lynn Dadd   *Toxic Free: How to Protect Your Health and Home from the Chemicals That Are Making You Sick.* New York: Jeremy P. Tarcher, 2011.

T.S.S. Dikshith   *Hazardous Chemicals: Safety Management and Global Regulations.* Boca Raton, FL: CRC Press, 2013.

Courtney Marie Dowdall and Ryan J. Klotz   *Pesticides and Global Health: Understanding Agrochemical Dependence and Investing in Sustainable Solutions.* Walnut Creek, CA: Left Coast Press, 2013.

Samuel S. Epstein with Randall Fitzgerald — *Toxic Beauty: How Cosmetics and Personal-Care Products Endanger Your Health . . . And What You Can Do About It*. Dallas, TX: BenBella Books, 2009.

Christina A. Farrugia, ed. — *Dispersant and Oil Monitoring in the Deepwater Horizon Spill*. Hauppauge, NY: Nova Science Publishers, 2011.

Merv Fingas — *The Basics of Oil Spill Cleanup*. 3rd ed. Boca Raton, FL: CRC Press, 2012.

Susan Freinkel — *Plastic: A Toxic Love Story*. New York: Houghton Mifflin Harcourt, 2011.

Russell Gold — *The Boom: How Fracking Ignited the American Energy Revolution and Changed the World*. New York: Simon & Schuster, 2014.

John Graves — *Fracking: America's Alternative Energy Revolution*. Ventura, CA: Safe Harbor International Publishing, 2012.

Thomas E. Higgins, Jayanti A. Sachdev, and Stephen A. Engleman — *Toxic Chemicals: Risk Prevention Through Use Reduction*. Boca Raton, FL: CRC Press, 2011.

Antonia Juhasz — *Black Tide: The Devastating Impact of the Gulf Oil Spill*. Hoboken, NJ: John Wiley & Sons, 2011.

Steve Lerner — *Sacrifice Zones: The Front Lines of Toxic Chemical Exposure in the United States*. Cambridge, MA: MIT Press, 2010.

Bruce Lourie and Rick Smith	*Toxin Toxout: Getting Harmful Chemicals Out of Our Bodies and Our World.* New York: St. Martin's Press, 2014.
Okon Obo	*Hydraulic Fracturing (Fracking): Procedures, Issues, and Benefits.* Houston, TX: Petroleum Zones, 2013.
Monona Rossol	*Pick Your Poison: How the Mad Dash to Chemical Utopia Is Making Lab Rats of Us All.* Hoboken, NJ: John Wiley & Sons, 2011.
James Salzman	*Drinking Water: A History.* New York: Overlook Press, 2012.
Michael SanClements	*Plastic Purge: How to Use Less Plastic, Eat Better, Keep Toxins Out of Your Body, and Help Save the Sea Turtles!* New York: St. Martin's Griffin, 2014.
Philip Shabecoff and Alice Shabecoff	*Poisoned for Profit: How Toxins Are Making Our Children Chronically Ill.* White River Junction, VT: Chelsea Green Publishing, 2010.
Rick Smith	*Electronic Cigarettes and Vaping: E-Cig Revolution: How to Save a Million Lives and a Billion Healthcare Dollars.* Seattle, WA: CreateSpace, 2013.
Jennifer Taggart	*Smart Mama's Green Guide: Simple Steps to Reduce Your Child's Toxic Chemical Exposure.* New York: Center Street, 2009.

Stephen M. Testa and James A. Jacobs	*Oil Spills and Gas Leaks: Environmental Response, Prevention, and Cost Recovery.* New York: McGraw-Hill, 2014.
Sarah A. Vogel	*Is It Safe?: BPA and the Struggle to Define the Safety of Chemicals.* Berkeley: University of California Press, 2012.
Zhendi Wang and Scott A. Stout	*Oil Spill Environmental Forensics: Fingerprinting and Source Identification.* Burlington, MA: Academic Press, 2010.

Index

A

Abrams, Lindsay, 111

Accidents. *See* Chemical spills; Explosions; Industrial accidents; Oil spills; Transportation

Accountability. *See* Transparency and accountability

Aflatoxin, 167–168

Aggregate exposure, 184–185
   See also Exposure levels and dosages

Air pollution
   chemical manufacturing and accidents, 203–204
   created, oil spill cleanup, 137, 143
   emissions rules, 131, 132
   fracking, 115, 117, 131
   populations affected, 37–38, 39

"Alarmism" regarding chemicals, 29–36, 163, 164, 165, 166–170, 171

Almonds, 167–168

American Academy of Pediatrics, 33–35, 184

American Chemistry Council, 24, 27, 49, 52, 71, 114, 195, 200

American Cleaning Institute, 52

American Council on Science, 24–25

American Dental Association, 165

American Lung Association, 61

American Petroleum Institute, 114, 115

America's Natural Gas Alliance, 114

"America's New Energy Future: The Unconventional Oil and Gas Revolution and the US Economy" (report), 113

Ammonium nitrate, 156–157

Amphibians
   animal testing, herbicides, 102, 169–170
   pesticide harms and die-offs, 100, 101–103

Anhydrous ammonia, 156–157, 203

Animal die-offs, 100–101, 102, 103, 105–107

Animal testing
   BPA, 199, 200
   herbicide effects, 102, 169–170
   published research, 24

Animal wastes, 78

Antibiotics, animal feeds, 78

Antimicrobial peptides, 103

Antimony, 37, 39

Aquatic wildlife
   cosmetics water pollution, 86
   oil spills and dispersant, harms, 134–135, 137–139, 141, 142–143, 144, 146–147, 148–149, 152–153
   pharmaceutical water pollution, 75, 76, 80–81

Arkansas
   earthquakes, 129
   fracking, 123, 129

N

O